The New Spaghetti Cookbook

Delicious Spaghetti Recipes for Pasta Lovers

By
BookSumo Press

Published by
http://www.booksumo.com

LEGAL NOTES

Table of Contents

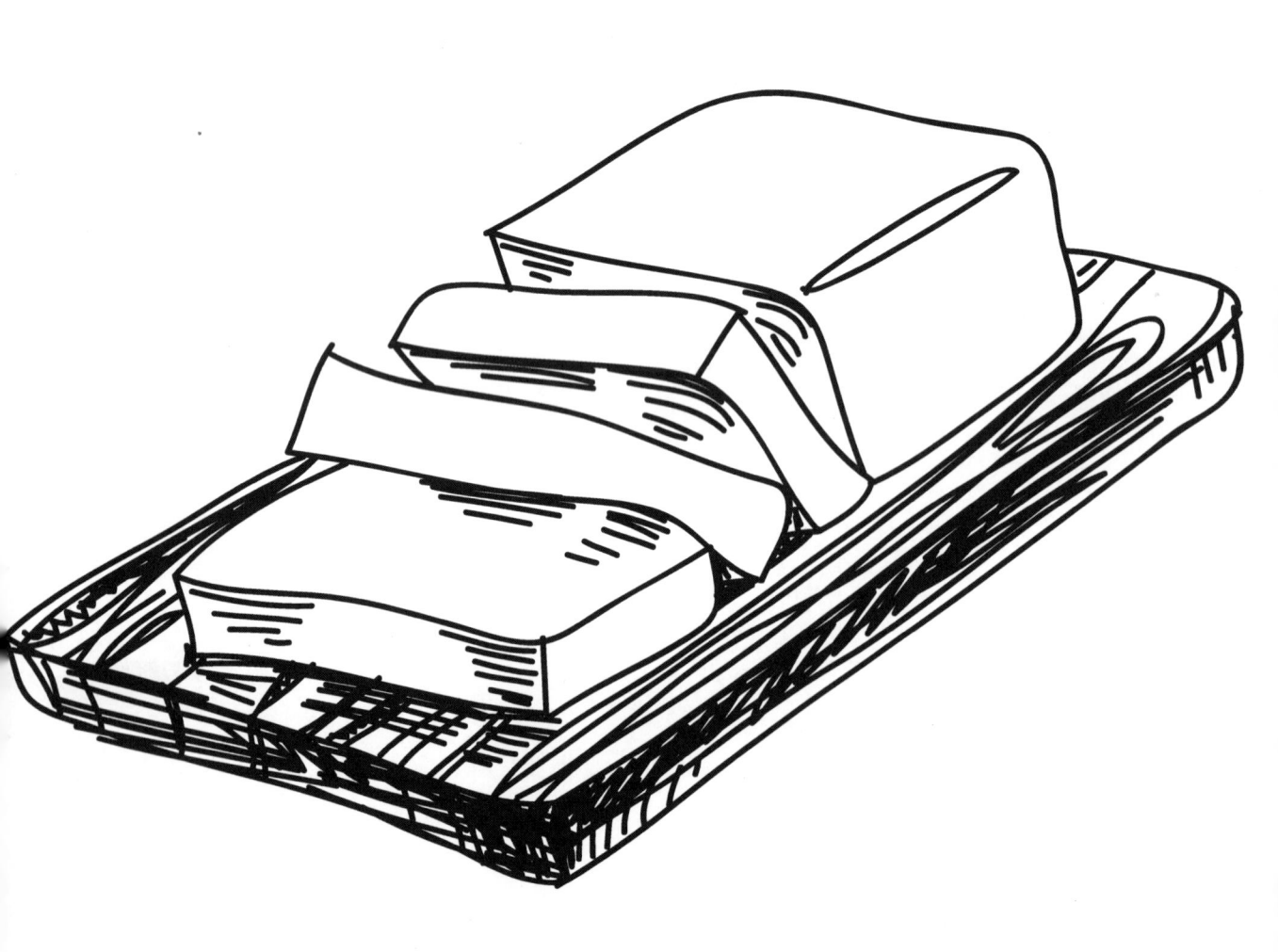

Southern Greek
Spaghetti

Prep Time: 10 mins
Total Time: 25 mins

Servings per Recipe: 4
Calories	313.2
Fat	12.3g
Cholesterol	30.5mg
Sodium	104.8mg
Carbohydrates	42.5g
Protein	7.5g

Ingredients

1/2 C. grated mizithra cheese
8 oz. spaghetti
4 tbsp butter
2 tsp minced garlic
2 tsp oregano

fresh ground black pepper

Directions

1. Prepare the pasta by following the instructions on the package until it becomes al dente.
2. Pour it in a colander and let it sit for few minutes.
3. Place a large skillet over medium heat. Heat in it the butter until it melt and become golden brown.
4. Add the spaghetti and stir to coat it with the melted butter. Stir in the cheese with garlic and oregano, a pinch of salt and pepper.
5. Serve your spaghetti warm.
6. Enjoy.

SPAGHETTI
Squash Spaghetti

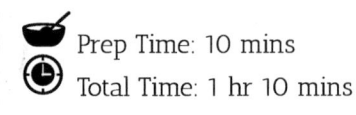
Prep Time: 10 mins
Total Time: 1 hr 10 mins

Servings per Recipe: 4
Calories   179.0
Fat   15.5g
Cholesterol   41.5mg
Sodium   305.3mg
Carbohydrates   5.7g
Protein   5.4g

Ingredients

1 medium spaghetti squash
1/2 C. grated parmesan cheese
1/4-1/2 C. butter

salt and pepper

Directions

1. Before you do anything, preheat the oven to 350 F.
2. Use a sharp knife or a fork to pierce the squash several times. Place it in a baking sheet.
3. Place the squash pan in the oven and let it cook for 65 min until it becomes soft.
4. Once the time is up, take out the squash from the oven and let it sit for few minutes to cool down.
5. Slice it in half then discard the seeds. Use a fork the scrap the squash pulp.
6. Get a mixing bowl: Mix in it the squash spaghetti with butter, cheese, a pinch of salt and pepper.
7. Garnish the spaghetti with some fresh oregano then serve it.
8. Enjoy.

Spaghetti Caprese

🥣 Prep Time: 8 mins

🕐 Total Time: 28 mins

Servings per Recipe: 1

Calories	587.6
Fat	15.6g
Cholesterol	0.0mg
Sodium	16.6mg
Carbohydrates	95.2g
Protein	16.6g

Ingredients

1 C. fresh tomato, diced
1 tbsp onion, minced
1 tbsp olive oil, divided
1/2 tsp sugar
1 tbsp fresh basil, chopped

salt,
1 pinch pepper
4 oz. spaghetti

Directions

1. Prepare the pasta by following the instructions on the package.
2. Place a large saucepan over medium heat. Heat in it 1/2 tbsp of oil. Sauté in it the onion for 2 min.
3. Lower the heat then stir in the tomatoes, sugar, pepper and salt. Let them cook for 6 min.
4. Stir in the basil with 1/2 tbsp of oil to the sauce. Mix them well. Turn off the heat and let it sit for few minutes.
5. Spoon the sauce over the spaghetti then serve it warm.
6. Enjoy.

PESTO
Aioli Dressing

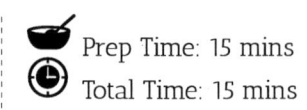 Prep Time: 15 mins

Total Time: 15 mins

Servings per Recipe: 20	
Calories	124.5
Fat	12.3g
Cholesterol	3.9mg
Sodium	157.9mg
Carbohydrates	3.4g
Protein	0.6g

Ingredients

3/4 C. oil
1 C. mayonnaise
3/4 C. buttermilk
2 tbsp grated Romano cheese
2 tbsp dried basil
1/2 tsp salt

1 clove garlic, minced
hot pepper sauce
1/4 tsp paprika

Directions

1. Get a small mixing bowl: Mix in it the mayo with oil.
2. Pour in the buttermilk, cheese, basil, salt, garlic, and hot pepper sauce. Whisk them until they become creamy.
3. Cover the bowl with a plastic wrap and let it sit for at least 8 h.
4. Once the time is up, Toss the spaghetti with the pesto sauce. Garnish it with some fresh basil.
5. Enjoy.

Olivia's
Tomato Sauce

Prep Time: 30 mins
Total Time: 1 hr 5 mins

Servings per Recipe: 6
Calories	210.8
Fat	18.5g
Cholesterol	0.0mg
Sodium	207.3mg
Carbohydrates	11.2g
Protein	2.5g

Ingredients

8 large fresh tomatoes, diced
1/2 C. olive oil
8 cloves fresh garlic, chopped
3/4 C. fresh basil, minced
1/2 tsp salt

1 tsp fresh ground black pepper
1/4 tsp crushed red pepper flakes

Directions

1. Place a pan over medium heat. Heat in it the oil. Cook in it the garlic for 1 min.
2. Stir in the tomatoes and cook them for 5 min. Add the basil with red pepper, a pinch of salt and pepper.
3. Let the sauce cook for 6 to 10 min over low heat until it becomes slightly thick.
4. Pour the some of the sauce over the spaghetti then serve it warm.
5. Enjoy.

SLOW COOKER
Spaghetti

Prep Time: 10 mins
Total Time: 6 hrs 10 mins

Servings per Recipe: 6
Calories	273.6
Fat	11.8g
Cholesterol	51.4mg
Sodium	966.5mg
Carbohydrates	23.5g
Protein	18.7g

Ingredients

1 lb. ground beef
2 tbsp instant minced onion
1 tsp salt
1/2 tsp garlic powder
8 oz. tomato sauce
1 1/2 tsp Italian seasoning

4 oz. mushrooms
3 C. tomato juice
4 oz. spaghetti, broken into pieces

Directions

1. Place a crock pot over medium heat. Cook in it the beef for 6 min.
2. Stir in the onion with tomato sauce, mushroom, tomato juice, Italian seasoning, garlic powder and salt.
3. Put on the lid and let them cook for 7 h on low.
4. Once the time is up, add the pasta. Put on the lid and let it cook for 60 min on high.
5. Enjoy.

Carbonara
Spaghetti

🥣 Prep Time: 5 mins
🕐 Total Time: 15 mins

Servings per Recipe: 4
Calories	860.4
Fat	52.6g
Cholesterol	273.1mg
Sodium	541.2mg
Carbohydrates	69.7g
Protein	26.4g

Ingredients

12 oz. spaghetti
1 tbsp olive oil
1 onion, chopped
4 oz. bacon, diced
1 clove garlic, chopped

3 eggs
1 1/4 C. heavy cream
2 oz. parmesan cheese
salt and pepper

Directions

1. Prepare the pasta by following the instructions on the package.
2. Place a pan over medium heat. Heat in it the oil. Cook in it the bacon with onion for 6 min.
3. Add the garlic and cook them for 1 min.
4. Get a mixing bowl: Whisk in it the eggs with cream, a pinch of salt and pepper.
5. Add them to the onion and bacon mixture. Stir them well and let them cook for 3 to 5 min over low heat.
6. Add the pasta to the sauce and stir it to a coat.
7. Adjust the seasoning of the pasta then serve it warm.
8. Enjoy.

CHINESE
Spaghetti

Prep Time: 20 mins
Total Time: 38 mins

Servings per Recipe: 6
Calories	337.1
Fat	9.5g
Cholesterol	48.4mg
Sodium	477.5mg
Carbohydrates	38.9g
Protein	22.7g

Ingredients

8 oz. spaghetti, uncooked
1 tbsp cornstarch
4 tbsp reduced sodium soy sauce, divided
2 tbsp sesame oil, divided
1 lb. boneless skinless chicken breast, cut into pieces
2 tbsp white vinegar
1 tbsp sugar

1 tbsp canola oil
2 C. fresh snow peas
2 C. carrots, shredded
3 green onions, chopped
3/8 tsp ground ginger, minced
1/2 tsp crushed red pepper flakes

Directions

1. Prepare the pasta by following the instructions on the package.
2. Get a mixing bowl: Mix in it the cornstarch and 1 tbsp soy sauce. Stir in 1 tbsp of sesame oil to make the marinade.
3. Place the chicken in a zip lock bag. Pour over it the sesame oil sauce. Press the bag to seal it and shake it to coat.
4. Place it aside and let it absorb the flavors for 12 min.
5. Get a mixing bowl: Mix in it vinegar, sugar, remaining soy sauce and sesame oil to make the sauce.
6. Place a large pan over medium heat. Heat in it the canola oil. Add the marinated chicken and cook it for 7 to 10 min until it is done.
7. Drain the chicken and place it aside. Add the carrots with peas then cook them for 6 min.
8. Stir in the green onions, ginger, and pepper flakes. Let them cook for 6 to 7 min until they are done to your liking.
9. Stir in the cooked chicken with vinegar sauce and spaghetti. Cook them for 2 min. Serve your chicken and spaghetti stir fry warm. Enjoy.

Pasta
Sausage Skillet

Prep Time: 5 mins
Total Time: 30 mins

Servings per Recipe: 4
Calories	400.4
Fat	15.6g
Cholesterol	58.4mg
Sodium	805.7mg
Carbohydrates	42.2g
Protein	22.9g

Ingredients

1/2 lb. lean ground beef
1/4 lb. bulk Italian sausage
2 (8 oz.) cans no-salt-added tomato sauce
1 (14 1/2 oz.) cans stewed tomatoes
1 C. water
1 (4 oz.) cans mushroom stems and pieces, drained

2 celery ribs, sliced
4 oz. uncooked spaghetti, broken in half
1/4 tsp dried oregano
salt and pepper

Directions

1. Place a pan over medium heat. Brown in it the sausage with beef for 8 min. Discard the fat.
2. Stir in the rest of the ingredients. Cook them until they start boiling. Put on the lid and let them cook for 15 to 17 min.
3. Serve you pasta pan warm. Garnish it with some chopped herbs.
4. Enjoy.

GILROY
Garlic Spaghetti

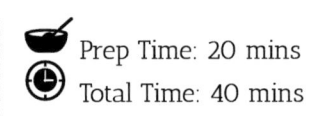

Prep Time: 20 mins

Total Time: 40 mins

Servings per Recipe: 2	
Calories	730.8
Fat	30.8g
Cholesterol	165.0mg
Sodium	441.9mg
Carbohydrates	88.9g
Protein	23.8g

Ingredients

8 oz. spaghetti
1 raw egg
5 - 8 cloves garlic, peeled and press
4 tbsp butter
1/4-1/3 C. grated parmesan cheese
1 tsp dried sweet basil leaves
1/4 C. chopped parsley

fresh ground black pepper
red pepper flakes
vegetarian bacon bits
parmesan cheese
black pepper

Directions

1. Prepare the pasta by following the instructions on the package until it becomes dente.
2. Get a food blender: Combine in it the egg, garlic, butter, grated Parmesan cheese and dried sweet basil. Blend them smooth to make the sauce
3. Get a serving bowl: Toss in it the pasta with the garlic sauce.
4. Adjust the seasoning if the spaghetti sauce. Serve it with some garlic bread.
5. Enjoy.

30-Minute
Spaghetti Skillet

🥣 Prep Time: 15 mins
🕐 Total Time: 30 mins

Servings per Recipe: 4
Calories   486.6
Fat   12.5g
Cholesterol   80.4mg
Sodium   515.2mg
Carbohydrates   60.4g
Protein   32.1g

Ingredients

1 lb. ground turkey
2 garlic cloves, minced
1 small green pepper, chopped
1 small onion, chopped
2 C. water
1 (28 oz.) jars traditional style spaghetti sauce

1/2 tsp red pepper flakes
8 oz. uncooked spaghetti, broken into thirds
parmesan cheese

Directions

1. Place a large saucepan over medium heat. Cook in it the turkey with garlic, onion and green pepper for 8 min.
2. Add the water with hot pepper flakes, spaghetti sauce, a pinch of salt and pepper.
3. Cook them until they start boiling. Add the spaghetti to the pot.
4. Bring it to a rolling boil for 14 to 16 min or until the pasta is done.
5. Get a mixing bowl:
6. Enjoy.

AUTUMN
Vegetable Roast

Prep Time: 45 mins
Total Time: 2 hrs 5 mins

Servings per Recipe: 6
Calories	285.7
Fat	16.6g
Cholesterol	43.7mg
Sodium	515.7mg
Carbohydrates	16.2g
Protein	19.3g

Ingredients

1 spaghetti squash
1 large carrot, sliced on the diagonal
2 stalks celery, sliced on the diagonal
1 large yellow onion, diced
1 red bell pepper, peeled, seeded and diced
2 tbsp extra virgin olive oil
28 oz. tomatoes, diced, peel and seed)
red pepper flakes, minced
1 tsp dried basil

1/2 tsp dried oregano
1 pinch ground allspice
3 garlic cloves, chopped
3/4 lb. part-skim mozzarella cheese
1/2 C. grated parmesan cheese
Oil

Directions

1. Put a large pot of water over high heat. Add to it the whole squash and let it cook until it starts boiling.
2. Put on the lid and keep it boiling for 55 min.
3. Place a large pan over medium heat. Heat in it a splash oil. Cook in it the onion with carrot for 6 min.
4. Stir in the rest of the celery with bell pepper, pepper flakes, a pinch of salt and pepper.
5. Cook them for 12 min while stirring them often. Stir in the remaining ingredients.
6. Let the sauce cook for 16 min over low heat. Add the mozzarella with parmesan cheese. Turn off the heat.
7. Drain the squash from the water. Slice it in half and let it cool down completely.
8. Discard the seeds. Use a fork to scrap the squash pulp.
9. Before you do anything, preheat the oven to 350 F. Grease a casserole dish with a cooking spray.
10. Lay half of the spaghetti squash in the greased casserole. Spread over it half of the cheesy

veggies mixture.

11. Repeat the process with the remaining mixture. Place the casserole in the oven and let it cook for 32 min.

12. Allow the spaghetti casserole to sit for 5 min then serve it warm.

13. Enjoy.

HOW TO BAKE
Spaghetti

🥣 Prep Time: 30 mins
⏱ Total Time: 1 hr 10 mins

Servings per Recipe: 10
Calories   549.4
Fat   29.5g
Cholesterol   92.7mg
Sodium   1609.4mg
Carbohydrates   39.8g
Protein   31.7g

Ingredients

1 lb. lean ground beef, browned
1 C. onion
1/2 C. sweet red pepper, chopped
1/2 C. green pepper, chopped
4 -6 garlic cloves, minced
1 tbsp butter
2 (10 oz.) cans rotel
1 (14 1/2 oz.) cans diced tomatoes
8 oz. sliced fresh mushrooms
1 (4 oz.) cans sliced ripe olives, drained
1 1/2 tbsp dried basil
1 1/2 tbsp dried oregano

12 oz. cooked and drained spaghetti
2 C. shredded Mexican blend cheese
2 C. shredded cheddar cheese
1 C. parmesan cheese, shredded
2 (10 3/4 oz.) cans cream of mushroom soup
1/2 C. water
1 tsp salt
1/8 tsp fresh ground pepper
paprika

Directions

1. Before you do anything, preheat the oven to 350 F.
2. Place a pan over medium heat. Heat in it 1 tbsp of butter. Cook in it the onion with garlic and pepper for 5 min.
3. Stir in the tomatoes, mushrooms, olives, hamburger meat, basil, oregano, salt and pepper. Cook them for 12 to 16 min.
4. Lay half of spaghetti in a casserole dish. Spread it over it half of the meat mixture followed by 2 C. of fiesta blend cheese.
5. Repeat the process to make another layer. Sprinkle the parmesan cheese on top.
6. Get a mixing bowl: Combine in it the soup with water. Pour it all over the spaghetti casserole.
7. Place the casserole in the oven and let it cook for 36 to 42 min.
8. Once the time is up, allow the casserole to sit for 5 min. Serve it warm. Enjoy.

Rosa's
Pasta Salad

🍳 Prep Time: 10 mins
🕐 Total Time: 20 mins

Servings per Recipe: 4	
Calories	350.1
Fat	6.5g
Cholesterol	22.2mg
Sodium	286.0mg
Carbohydrates	58.1g
Protein	13.9g

Ingredients

250 g spaghetti
1/3 C. peas, frozen
10 cherry tomatoes, quartered
100 g feta cheese
2 tsp pesto sauce
1 tbsp fresh rosemary, minced
1/8 tsp granulated garlic

1/2 tbsp fresh chives, minced
1 tsp oil
fresh ground black pepper

Directions

1. Prepare the pasta by following the instructions on the package for 9 min.
2. Stir in the peas and cook them for an extra 2 to 3 min.
3. Pour the spaghetti and peas in a colander. Let them drain for few minutes.
4. Get a mixing bowl: Toss in it the spaghetti with oil and pesto sauce.
5. Add the herbs, garlic, pepper and salt. Combine them well. Stir in the feta cheese with cherry tomatoes.
6. Place the salad in the fridge and let it sit for at least 1 h then serve it.
7. Enjoy

SUNNY
Squash Gratin

Prep Time: 10 mins
Total Time: 40 mins

Servings per Recipe: 6
Calories   129.5
Fat   11.0g
Cholesterol   30.0mg
Sodium   116.6mg
Carbohydrates   5.3g
Protein   3.2g

Ingredients

1 medium spaghetti squash
2 tbsp butter
1 small yellow onion, halved and sliced
1/4 tsp red pepper flakes
1 tsp fresh thyme

1/2 C. sour cream
1/2 C. shredded cheddar cheese

Directions

1. Before you do anything, preheat the oven to 375 F.
2. Slice the squash in half. Discard the seeds. Place it a baking dish. Fill 1/4 inch of the dish with water.
3. Place the squash dish in the microwave and let it cook for 12 min on high.
4. Once the time is up, drain the spaghetti squash. Use a fork to scrap the spaghetti.
5. Get a mixing bowl: Toss in it the spaghetti squash with onions, sour cream and half the cheese.
6. Pour the mixture into a casserole dish. Sprinkle over it the remaining cheese.
7. Place the spaghetti casserole in the oven. Let it cook for 16 to 21 min. Serve it warm.
8. Enjoy.

Monterey Turkey and Pasta Bake

Prep Time: 5 mins
Total Time: 1 hr 25 mins

Servings per Recipe: 4
Calories   346.7
Fat   13.2g
Cholesterol   20.2mg
Sodium   1232.0mg
Carbohydrates   42.5g
Protein   14.0g

Ingredients

1 medium onion, chopped
1 medium carrot, chopped
1 celery rib, chopped
1/3 C. fresh mushrooms, sliced
1 tbsp butter
2 1/2 C. chicken broth
1 (10 3/4 oz.) cans condensed cream of mushroom soup

1/4 tsp salt
1/4 tsp pepper
2 1/2 C. cooked turkey breast, cubed
6 oz. spaghetti, Uncooked and broken in pieces
1/2 C. Monterey jack cheese, shredded
1/2 tsp paprika

Directions

1. Before you do anything, preheat the oven to 350 F.
2. Place a skillet over medium heat. Heat in it the butter until it melts.
3. Cook in it the celery with onion, carrot, and mushroom for 6 to 7 min until they become soft.
4. Get a mixing bowl: Whisk in it the broth, soup, salt and pepper.
5. Spread the turkey in the bottom of a baking dish. Top it with the spaghetti, and cooked veggies mixture.
6. Drizzle all over it the broth mixture. Lay a loose piece of foil over the dish to cover it.
7. Place the casserole in the oven and let it cook for 75 to 82 min.
8. Once the time is up, discard the foil. Sprinkle the cheese on top. Bake the casserole for an extra 6 to 11 min.
9. Serve your spaghetti casserole warm.
10. Enjoy.

PEPPERY
Glazed Spaghetti

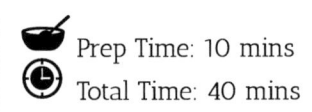

Prep Time: 10 mins
Total Time: 40 mins

Servings per Recipe: 4
Calories	422.7
Fat	7.9g
Cholesterol	7.6mg
Sodium	29.1mg
Carbohydrates	77.1g
Protein	13.0g

Ingredients

1 tbsp extra virgin olive oil
1 tbsp butter
3 cloves garlic, chopped
1 C. chopped red onion
3 sweet red peppers, seeded, chopped
1 1/3 C. vegetable stock
salt

fresh ground pepper
3/4 lb. spaghetti
1/2 C. chopped fresh basil
1 large lemon, grated zest of
grated parmesan cheese

Directions

1. Prepare the spaghetti by following the instructions on the package. Drain it.
2. Place a pan over high heat. Heat in it the oil with butter. Sauté in it the garlic, onion, and red peppers for 6 min.
3. Stir in the stock with a pinch of salt and pepper. Put on the lid and let them cook for 10 to 12 min over low heat.
4. Get a food blender: Pour in it the cooked veggies mixture. Blend them smooth.
5. Pour the mixture back into the pan. Let them cook for 9 min over low heat until the sauce becomes thick.
6. Stir the spaghetti with basil, a pinch of salt and pepper into the sauce.
7. Serve you spaghetti warm with some garlic bread.
8. Enjoy.

Oriental
Spaghetti Squash

Prep Time: 20 mins
Total Time: 35 mins

Servings per Recipe: 4
Calories	332.4
Fat	21.4g
Cholesterol	0.0mg
Sodium	429.5mg
Carbohydrates	30.1g
Protein	10.9g

Ingredients

1(3 lb.) spaghetti squash
1/3 C. sesame seeds
1 vegetable bouillon cube
1/3-1/2 C. hot water
2 tbsp reduced sodium soy sauce
1 tbsp sugar
2 tsp sesame oil
1 tsp cornstarch
1 tsp red pepper flakes

1 tsp Worcestershire sauce
1 - 2 tsp peanut oil
2 medium carrots, julienned
1 large red bell pepper, seeded and sliced
1/2 lb. fresh asparagus, trimmed and cut on the diagonal
1/3 C. chopped peanuts
1/3 C. minced fresh cilantro

Directions

1. Use a fork or a knife to pierce the squash all over. Put in the microwave and cook it for 6 min on high pressure.

2. Flip the squash and cook it for an extra 5 to 6 min on high. Place it aside to cool down.

3. Place a large skillet over medium heat. Toast in it the sesame seeds 40 sec. Get a food processor: Combine in it the sesame seeds with vegetable cube, hot water, soy sauce, sugar, and sesame oil.

4. Add the cornstarch, red pepper flakes and Worcestershire sauce. Blend them smooth to make the sauce.

5. Heat the oil in the pan. Cook in it the asparagus for 2 to 3 min. Stir in the carrots and cook them for 2 min.

6. Stir in the bell pepper and cook them for an extra 3 min. Add the sesame seeds sauce. Let them cook for 2 min to make the sauce.

7. Use a fork to scrap the pulp of the squash. Place the spaghetti on serving plate. Drizzle over it the sauce then serve it.

8. Enjoy.

SONOMA
Roasted Spaghetti and Spinach

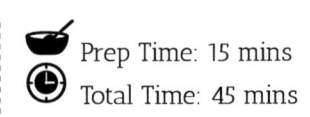

Prep Time: 15 mins
Total Time: 45 mins

Servings per Recipe: 2	
Calories	774.3
Fat	31.4g
Cholesterol	138.1mg
Sodium	1469.3mg
Carbohydrates	65.6g
Protein	57.9g

Ingredients

4 oz. spaghetti
2 boneless skinless chicken breast halves, cut in pieces
1 tbsp olive oil
3 garlic cloves, smashed
1/2 C. red onion, chopped
2 C. packed fresh spinach
Base
1 (14 oz.) cans stewed tomatoes (Italian style)
1/2 tsp dried basil
1/2 tsp dried tarragon
1 dash salt
1/4 tsp crushed red pepper flakes
2 tbsp fresh parsley
2 garlic cloves
1/2 C. grated parmesan cheese
Garnishings
1/4 C. parmesan cheese
1/2 C. sharp cheddar cheese

Directions

1. Before you do anything, preheat the oven to 400 F.
2. Prepare the spaghetti by following the instructions on the package. Drain it.
3. Place a pot over medium heat. Heat in it the oil. Cook in it the onion with garlic for 3 min.
4. Stir in the chicken and cook them for 5 min.
5. Get a blender: Combine in it the stewed tomatoes, basil, tarragon, salt, chili flakes, parsley, garlic and cheese. Blend them until they become chunky.
6. Stir the mixture into the chicken pan. Cook them over low medium heat for 16 min.
7. Lay the spinach in the bottom of a baking dish. Top it with the spaghetti. Spread over them the chicken mixture followed by cheese.
8. Season the spaghetti casserole with a pinch of chili flakes. Cook it in the oven for 25 to 32 min.
9. Allow the spaghetti dish to rest for 5 min then serve it.
10. Enjoy.

Hudson
Parmesan Bake

Prep Time: 15 mins
Total Time: 1 hr 5 mins

Servings per Recipe: 4
Calories   222.1
Fat   13.3g
Cholesterol   59.1mg
Sodium   371.0mg
Carbohydrates   13.9g
Protein   12.1g

Ingredients

1 (10 oz.) packages frozen chopped spinach
1 egg, slightly beaten
1/2 C. sour cream
1/2 C. milk
2 tbsp grated parmesan cheese
1/2 small onion, chopped
1/2 tsp salt
black pepper,
2 C. Monterey jack cheese, shredded
4 oz. angel hair pasta

Directions

1. Before you do anything, preheat the oven to 16 min. Grease a baking dish with a cooking spray.
2. Prepare the spaghetti by following the instructions on the package. Drain it.
3. Place the spinach in some hot water until it wilts. Drain it.
4. Get a mixing bowl: Mix in it the egg, sour cream, milk, Parmesan cheese, chopped onion, salt, black pepper, and Monterey Jack cheese.
5. Stir in the spaghetti with spinach. Pour the mixture into the greased dish.
6. Lay a piece of foil over it to cover it. Place the dish in the oven and let it cook for 16 min.
7. Once the time is up, discard the oil and let the casserole cook for an extra 46 min.
8. Allow the spaghetti bake to sit for 5 min then serve it warm.
9. Enjoy.

PARK AVE
Pizza Casserole

Prep Time: 10 mins
Total Time: 40 mins

Servings per Recipe: 8
Calories	262.8
Fat	9.8g
Cholesterol	72.0mg
Sodium	413.6mg
Carbohydrates	29.7g
Protein	12.9g

Ingredients

8 oz. spaghetti
2 eggs
1/2 C. milk
1 can your favorite spaghetti sauce
1 can of diced tomatoes with garlic
1 (8 oz.) packages shredded mozzarella cheese
Garnish
onion

green pepper
pepperoni
sausage
mushroom
fresh basil
pizza seasoning
parmesan cheese

Directions

1. Before you do anything, preheat the oven to 350 F.
2. Prepare the spaghetti by following the instructions on the package for 6 min. Drain it.
3. Get a mixing bowl: Toss in the spaghetti with milk, egg, a pinch of salt and pepper.
4. Pour the mixture into a greased casserole dish. Spread over it the spaghetti sauce followed by the tomato.
5. Sprinkle the cheese on top followed by your favorite pizza toppings.
6. Place the casserole in the oven and let it cook for 26 to 32 min.
7. Allow the spaghetti casserole to sit for 5 min then serve it warm.
8. Enjoy.

Italian Style
Sausage and Pasta Casserole

🥘 Prep Time: 30 mins
🕐 Total Time: 1 hr 10 mins

Servings per Recipe: 12	
Calories	533.3
Fat	28.5g
Cholesterol	65.9mg
Sodium	1217.9mg
Carbohydrates	42.9g
Protein	27.1g

Ingredients

2 lbs. mild Italian sausage, casings removed
2 onions, chopped
6 garlic cloves, minced
1 tbsp dried basil
4 C. sliced mushrooms
2 (28 oz.) cans chopped tomatoes
1 (5 1/2 oz.) cans tomato paste
1/2 tsp pepper
6 C. chopped fresh spinach
1 (12 oz.) packages spaghetti

Garnish
2 tbsp butter
1/2 C. all-purpose flour
3 C. milk
3/4 C. shredded mozzarella cheese
1/8 tsp salt
1/8 tsp fresh ground black pepper
1/2 C. grated parmesan cheese

Directions

1. Before you do anything, preheat the oven to 375 F.
2. To make the sauce:
3. Prepare the spaghetti by following the instructions on the package.
4. Before you do anything, preheat the oven to 450 F. Grease a baking sheet and place it aside.
5. Place a pot over medium heat. Cook in it the sausage for 6 min. Stir in the onions, garlic and basil for 6 min.
6. Stir in the mushroom and cook them for 6 min. Stir in the tomatoes, tomato paste and pepper.
7. Cook them until they start boiling. Lower the heat and let them cook for 16 min.
8. Fold the spinach into the mixture to make the meat sauce.
9. Stir into it the spaghetti to coat it.
10. To make the topping:

11. Place a large saucepan over medium heat. Heat in it the butter until it melts.

12. Mix in the flour and let it cook for 60 seconds while mixing all the time. Add the milk gradually while mixing all the time.

13. Let them cook for 14 min while mixing them with a hand whisk until the sauce becomes thick.

14. Stir in the mozzarella cheese with a pinch of salt and pepper until it melts.

15. Pour the spaghetti into a greased baking dish. Pour over it the cheese sauce. Cover it with parmesan cheese.

16. Place the spaghetti casserole in the oven and let it cook for 32 to 42 min.

17. Once the time is up, allow the spaghetti casserole to sit for 5 min then serve it warm.

18. Enjoy.

Chipotle Spaghetti

Prep Time: 30 mins
Total Time: 50 mins

Servings per Recipe: 10
Calories	525.9
Fat	27.8g
Cholesterol	94.5mg
Sodium	835.7mg
Carbohydrates	37.5g
Protein	31.6g

Ingredients

12 oz. spaghetti, broken in thirds
2 lbs. ground beef
1 large onion, diced
1 (16 oz.) jars Pace Picante Sauce, Thick and Chunky
1 C. mexicorn, drained

1 (14 1/2 oz.) cans tomatoes, drained
2 (4 1/2 oz.) cans sliced black olives, drained
1 1/2 C. Monterey jack cheese, shredded
1 1/2 C. cheddar cheese, shredded

Directions

1. Prepare the spaghetti by following the instructions on the package.
2. Place a pot over high heat. Cook in it the beef with onion for 8 min. Discard the fat.
3. Stir in the spaghetti with picante sauce, Mexican corn, tomatoes, and olives.
4. Fold the cheddar and jack cheese into the mixture. Cook them for few minutes until the cheese melts.
5. Enjoy.

BLACK
Feta Spaghetti

Prep Time: 10 mins
Total Time: 30 mins

Servings per Recipe: 4
Calories   627.6
Fat   29.8g
Cholesterol   25.3mg
Sodium   793.9mg
Carbohydrates   74.0g
Protein   17.2g

Ingredients

1 1/2 lbs. tomatoes, seeded and chopped
1/2 C. kalamata olives, pitted
1/4 lb. feta cheese, crumbled
3 tbsp drained capers
3 tbsp parsley, chopped flat-leaf
1/4 tsp salt

1/4 tsp fresh ground black pepper
3/4 lb. spaghetti
6 tbsp olive oil
3 garlic cloves, minced

Directions

1. Prepare the spaghetti by following the instructions on the package.
2. Get a mixing bowl: Stir in it the tomatoes, olives, feta, capers, parsley, salt, and pepper.
3. Place a pan over medium heat. Heat in it the oil. Cook in it the garlic for 45 min.
4. Stir in spaghetti and toss it to coat. Add it the tomato mixture and mix them.
5. Chill the salad in the fridge for at least 35 min then serve it.
6. Enjoy.

A Blue-Collar
Lunch (Pasta and Ground Beef Sandwich)

Prep Time: 15 mins
Total Time: 30 mins

Servings per Recipe: 10
Calories	517.9
Fat	30.9g
Cholesterol	80.6mg
Sodium	599.3mg
Carbohydrates	44.0g
Protein	15.5g

Ingredients

1 lb. ground beef
1 tsp Italian seasoning
2 tbsp olive oil
1 (32 oz.) jars spaghetti sauce

1 (8 oz.) boxes spaghetti, cooked
1 loaf(20 slices) sliced white bread
1 C. butter, room temperature

Directions

1. Place a pot over high heat. Cook in it the beef for 9 min. Discard the fat.
2. Stir in the olive oil with spaghetti sauce. Cook them for 3 min. Stir in the spaghetti and cook them for an extra 2 min.
3. Spread the butter over the bread slices. Serve them with the warm spaghetti.
4. Enjoy.

OMELETS
Milanese

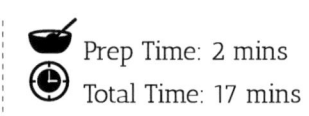 Prep Time: 2 mins
Total Time: 17 mins

Servings per Recipe: 2
Calories	891.3
Fat	53.8g
Cholesterol	539.3mg
Sodium	822.7mg
Carbohydrates	65.7g
Protein	34.9g

Ingredients

6 -8 oz. leftover spaghetti, with any
sauce
4 eggs
2 oz. grated parmesan cheese

3 oz. butter
salt & ground black pepper

Directions

1. Before you do anything, preheat the oven to 450 F. Grease a baking sheet and place it aside.
2. Get a mixing bowl: Mix in it the pasta, eggs and cheese, a pinch of salt and pepper.
3. Place a pan over medium heat. Melt in it 1.5 oz. of butter. Pour in it the spaghetti mixture.
4. Let it cook for 11 min until it sit. Use a plastic or thin spatula to loosen the frittata. Flip it into a plate.
5. Heat the remaining butte in the same pan. Slide into it the tart with the uncooked side facing down.
6. Let it cook for 2 to 4 min or until it is done. Serve it with some ketchup.
7. Enjoy.

Spaghetti
Naples
(Aglio Olio)

Prep Time: 20 mins
Total Time: 35 mins

Servings per Recipe: 4
CCalories   1284.7
Fat   27.7g
Cholesterol   345.6mg
Sodium   354.3mg
Carbohydrates   176.7g
Protein   76.7g

Ingredients

1 lb. ground beef
2 lbs. large shrimp, peeled and deveined
1 lemon, juice
1/4 C. chopped parsley
1 tsp crushed red pepper flakes
4 garlic cloves, peeled and crushed
salt
2 tbsp olive oil

1 lb. spaghetti
1/4 C. olive oil
1 (2 oz.) cans anchovy fillets
7 - 8 garlic cloves, minced
1/2 tsp crushed red pepper flakes
1/4 C. parsley,   chopped
salt

Directions

1. Prepare the spaghetti by following the instructions on the package until it becomes dente. To make the shrimp:

2. Get a mixing bowl: Combine in it the shrimp with lemon juice, parsley, pepper flakes, garlic, olive oil and a pinch of salt.

3. Place a pan over medium heat. Heat in it the oil. Cook in it the shrimp for 3 to 4 min or until it becomes pink.

4. Turn off the heat and put on the lid. Place it aside.

5. To make the spaghetti: Place a small skillet over medium heat. Heat 1/4 C. of olive oil in it. Cook in it the red pepper with garlic and anchovies for 2 min. Stir in the pasta and coat it with the mixture. Add the parsley and toss them to coat. Spoon the shrimp over the spaghetti then serve it warm.

6. Enjoy.

MEXICAN STYLE
Pasta Casserole

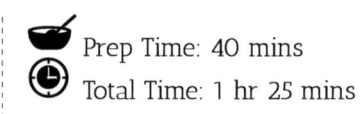

Prep Time: 40 mins
Total Time: 1 hr 25 mins

Servings per Recipe: 10
Calories 549.1
Fat 27.0g
Cholesterol 103.4mg
Sodium 1702.2mg
Carbohydrates 41.0g
Protein 35.6g

Ingredients

4 -5 C. cooked chicken, cut into pieces
1 C. yellow onion, chopped
1/2 C. red sweet bell pepper, chopped
1/2 C. green bell pepper, chopped
6 -8 garlic cloves, minced
1 tbsp butter
2 (10 oz.) cans Rotel Tomatoes
1 (8 oz.) cans tomato sauce
6 oz. sliced fresh mushrooms
1 (4 oz.) cans sliced ripe olives, drained
1 1/2 tbsp dried basil
1 1/2 tbsp dried oregano
12 oz. spaghetti, cooked, drained and
coated with olive oil
2 C. shredded Mexican blend cheese
1 1/4 C. shredded cheddar cheese
1 C. parmesan cheese, shredded
1 (10 3/4 oz.) cans cream of mushroom
soup
1 (10 3/4 oz.) cans cream of chicken
soup
1 (10 3/4 oz.) cans milk
1/4 C. water
1 tsp salt
1/8 tsp fresh ground pepper
paprika

Directions

1. Before you do anything, preheat the oven to 350 F.
2. Place a pan over medium heat. Heat in it 1 tbsp of butter. Cook in it the onion, peppers and garlic for 3 min.
3. Stir in the tomatoes, tomato sauce, mushrooms, olives, chicken, basil, oregano, salt and pepper. Cook them for 12 to 16 min to make the sauce.
4. Lay half of the pasta in the bottom of a casserole dish. Spread over it half of the meat sauce followed by 2 C. of cheese blend.
5. Repeat the process to make another layer. Sprinkle the parmesan and cheddar cheese on top.
6. Get a mixing bowl: Stir in it the milk with water and soups. Pour it all over the spaghetti casserole.
7. Place the pan in the oven and let it cook for 36 to 46 min. Serve it warm with some garlic bread.
8. Enjoy.

Thursday's
Lunch Box
(Pasta with Capers)

Prep Time: 6 mins
Total Time: 16 mins

Servings per Recipe: 4

Calories	641.8
Fat	6.1g
Cholesterol	14.3mg
Sodium	196.3mg
Carbohydrates	112.4g
Protein	31.9g

Ingredients

17.5 oz. spaghetti
6.5 cans tuna in olive oil, drained
15.5 oz. cans of peeled roma tomatoes,
diced
1 small white onion, diced

sea salt
crushed black peppercorns
capers
grated parmesan cheese

Directions

1. Prepare the pasta by following the instructions on the package.
2. Place a pan over medium heat. Heat in it a splash of oil. Cook in it the onion with tuna for 3 min.
3. Add the tomato and cook them for 3 min. Stir in the tuna with capers.
4. Divide the spaghetti between serving plates. Spoon over it the tuna mixture.
5. Sprinkle the cheese on top then serve them.
6. Enjoy.

SPAGHETTI
Kalamata

Prep Time: 20 mins
Total Time: 20 mins

Servings per Recipe: 4
Calories	627.5
Fat	29.8g
Cholesterol	25.3mg
Sodium	793.9mg
Carbohydrates	74.0g
Protein	17.2g

Ingredients

1 1/2 lbs. tomatoes, seeded and chopped
1/2 C. kalamata olives, pitted
1/4 lb. feta cheese, crumbled
3 tbsp capers, drained
3 tbsp flat leaf parsley, chopped
1/4 tsp salt

1/4 tsp fresh ground black pepper
3/4 lb. spaghetti
6 tbsp olive oil
3 garlic cloves, minced

Directions

1. Prepare the spaghetti by following the instructions on the package.
2. Get a mixing bowl: Combine in it the tomatoes, olives, feta, capers, parsley, salt, and pepper.
3. Place a pan over medium heat. Heat in it the oil. Cook in it the garlic for 60 seconds.
4. Stir in the spaghetti and toss them to coat. Add the tomato mixture and toss to coat.
5. Adjust the seasoning of the salad then let it chill in the fridge for at least 1 h.
6. Serve your salad with some garlic bread.
7. Enjoy.

Bella
Spaghetti

🥘 Prep Time: 5 mins
🕐 Total Time: 20 mins

Servings per Recipe: 4	
Calories	382.3
Fat	9.7g
Cholesterol	4.4mg
Sodium	101.5mg
Carbohydrates	61.2g
Protein	15.0g

Ingredients

9 oz. pasta
2 tbsp olive oil
6 garlic cloves, crushed
1 tsp red chile
2 spring onions, sliced
3 tsp rosemary, chopped

1 large zucchini, cut in half lengthways
5 large portabella mushrooms, sliced
15 to 16 oz. cans tomatoes
4 tbsp parmesan cheese
fresh ground black pepper

Directions

1. Prepare the spaghetti by following the instructions on the package. Drain it.
2. Place a pan over medium heat. Heat in it the oil. Cook in it the chili with onion and garlic for 3 min.
3. Stir in the rosemary with mushroom and zucchini. Cook them for 5 to 7 min until they become soft
4. Stir in the spaghetti. Adjust the seasoning of your spaghetti skillet then serve it warm.
5. Enjoy.

SIMPLE
Spaghetti with Garlic Oil

🥣 Prep Time: 15 mins
🕐 Total Time: 25 mins

Servings per Recipe: 4
Calories	585.2
Fat	19.7g
Cholesterol	0.0mg
Sodium	1751.5mg
Carbohydrates	85.8g
Protein	15.0g

Ingredients

1/3 C. extra virgin olive oil
2 large garlic cloves, minced
1 tbsp salt
1 lb. spaghetti

2 tbsp minced fresh flat-leaf parsley
crushed red pepper flakes

Directions

1. Prepare the spaghetti by following the instructions on the package. Drain it.
2. Combine the garlic with oil in a microwave safe bowl. Lay a piece parchment paper over it to cover it.
3. Place in the microwave and cook it for 2 min on high.
4. Get a mixing bowl: Toss in it the garlic and oil mix with parsley, spaghetti, a pinch of salt and pepper.
5. Serve your spaghetti warm or cold.
6. Enjoy.

Mediterranean Lentil Pasta Sauce

Prep Time: 10 mins
Total Time: 45 mins

Servings per Recipe: 6
Calories	161.2
Fat	3.1g
Cholesterol	0.0mg
Sodium	407.4mg
Carbohydrates	26.0g
Protein	9.4g

Ingredients

1 tbsp vegetable oil
1 onion, chopped
2 cloves garlic, minced
1 C. uncooked red lentil
2 C. water
1 (5 1/2 oz.) cans tomato paste

3/4 C. water
1 tbsp chopped fresh parsley
1/2 tsp dried oregano
1/2 tsp salt
1 pinch cayenne pepper

Directions

1. Place a pot over medium heat. Heat in it the oil. Cook in it the garlic with onion for 6 min.
2. Stir in the lentils with water, a pinch of salt and pepper. Put on the lid and let them cook for 25 to 35 min.
3. Stir in the tomato paste, 3/4 C. water and seasonings. Put on the lid and let them cook for an extra 12 to 16 min
4. Spoon the sauce over the spaghetti then serve it warm.
5. Enjoy.

JALAPENO
Spaghetti

Prep Time: 45 mins
Total Time: 45 mins

Servings per Recipe: 8
Calories	585.1
Fat	26.0g
Cholesterol	88.7mg
Sodium	731.6mg
Carbohydrates	54.6g
Protein	31.3g

Ingredients

1 lb. spaghetti
salt
1 tbsp extra virgin olive oil
3 slices bacon, chopped
1 lb. lean ground beef
1 medium onion, chopped
3 - 4 garlic cloves, chopped
fresh ground black pepper
2 tsp hot sauce
1 tbsp Worcestershire sauce
1 tbsp chili powder
1/2 tbsp ground cumin
5 oz. ale beer

14 oz. crushed fire-roasted tomatoes
8 oz. tomato sauce
2 tbsp butter
2 tbsp flour
1 C. chicken stock
1 C. milk
2 1/2 C. shredded cheddar cheese
1/4 C. pickled jalapeno pepper, chopped
4 scallions, chopped

Directions

1. Prepare the spaghetti by following the instructions on the package. Drain it.
2. To make the tomato sauce:
3. Place a large skillet over medium heat. Heat in it the oil. Cook in it the bacon for 6 min.
4. Drain it and place it aside.
5. Stir in the sirloin and cook it for 5 min. Stir in the garlic with onion, hot sauce, Worcestershire, chili powder and cumin, a pinch of salt and pepper.
6. Let them cook for 6 min. Stir in the beer and let them cook for 1 to 2 min.
7. Stir in the tomato with tomato sauce. Cook them until they start boiling for 6 min. Stir in the spaghetti.
8. To make the cheese sauce:
9. Heat in it the butter until it melts. Mix in the flour and cook it for 60 seconds.

10. Add the chicken stock while whisking them all the time followed by the milk. Let them cook for 2 to 3 min.
11. Add the cheese and stir it until it melts. Fold the scallions with jalapenos, a pinch of salt and pepper.
12. Divide the spaghetti between serving plates. Drizzle the cheese sauce on top then serve them right away.
13. Enjoy.

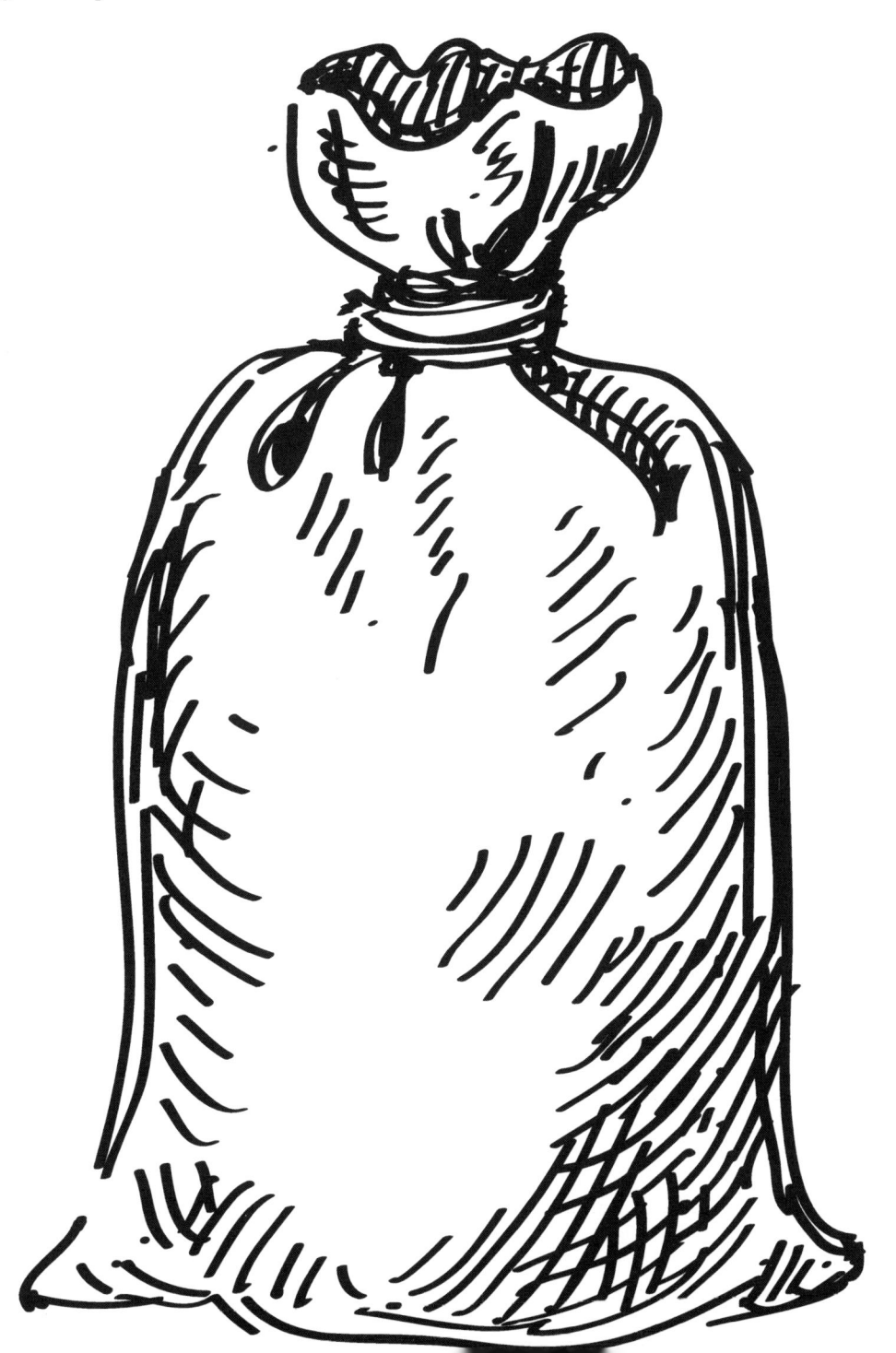

MULTI-GRAIN
Mushrooms Pasta

Prep Time: 15 mins
Total Time: 30 mins

Servings per Recipe: 8
Calories	130.5
Fat	8.7g
Cholesterol	15.6mg
Sodium	275.7mg
Carbohydrates	5.6g
Protein	8.4g

Ingredients

12 oz. multi-grain spaghetti
2 tbsp olive oil
8 garlic cloves, minced
2 tbsp basil
1 tbsp oregano
8 oz. sliced mushrooms

1 yellow pepper, sliced into matchsticks
1 pint grape tomatoes, sliced in halves
1 (14 oz.) cans Italian tomatoes
5 oz. parmesan cheese, grated

Directions

1. Prepare the spaghetti by following the instructions on the package. Drain it.
2. Place a pan over medium heat. Heat in it the oil. Cook in it the garlic, basil, and oregano for 12 min.
3. Stir in the mushrooms, pepper, and tomatoes. Cook them for 6 to 8 min.
4. Add the spaghetti and toss it to coat. Add the parmesan cheese and stir it until it melts.
5. Serve your spaghetti warm.
6. Enjoy.

Poppy Pasta and Sesame Salad

Prep Time: 10 mins
Total Time: 22 mins

Servings per Recipe: 4
Calories	683.1
Fat	22.8g
Cholesterol	0.0mg
Sodium	737.0mg
Carbohydrates	103.3g
Protein	17.3g

Ingredients

1 (16 oz.) packages spaghetti, broken in half
3 medium tomatoes, diced
1 cucumber, seeded and diced
1 green pepper, diced
1 red onion, diced
1 (10 oz.) bottles Italian salad dressing

1 tsp poppy seed
1/2 tsp paprika
1/4 tsp celery salt
1 tsp sesame seeds
1/8 tsp garlic salt

Directions

1. Prepare the spaghetti by following the instructions on the package. Drain it.
2. Get a mixing bowl: Toss in it the veggies with spaghetti.
3. Get a mixing bowl: Whisk in it the Italian dressing with poppy seed, paprika, celery salt, sesame seeds and garlic salt.
4. Add the dressing to the pasta then toss it to coat. Chill the salad in the fridge for few hours then serve it.
5. Enjoy.

CAMILLUS
Cheddar Pasta

Prep Time: 10 mins
Total Time: 30 mins

Servings per Recipe: 6
Calories	319.6
Fat	13.1g
Cholesterol	39.7mg
Sodium	485.6mg
Carbohydrates	35.3g
Protein	15.3g

Ingredients

1/2 lb. spaghetti
1/2 lb. sharp to old cheddar cheese, cubed
1 large onion, chopped
1 (19 oz.) cans tomato juice

butter
salt and pepper

Directions

1. Before you do anything, preheat the oven to 350 F.
2. Prepare the spaghetti by following the instructions on the package. Drain it.
3. Place a saucepan over medium heat. Heat in it the oil. Sauté in it the onion with a pinch of salt for 3 min.
4. Stir in the tomato juice. Cook them until they start boiling. Stir in the cheese until it melts.
5. Add the spaghetti and toss them to coat.
6. Pour the spaghetti mixture in a baking dish. Place it in the oven and let it cook for 12 min 16 min.
7. Enjoy.

80-Minute
Spaghetti Bolognese

Prep Time: 50 mins
Total Time: 1 hr 20 mins

Servings per Recipe: 8
Calories   589.8
Fat   22.5g
Cholesterol   82.7mg
Sodium   1053.9mg
Carbohydrates   62.6g
Protein   34.5g

Ingredients

1 lb. spaghetti, cooked
2 lbs. ground beef, cooked and drained
3 garlic cloves, diced
2 large onions, diced
1 green pepper, diced
2 celery ribs, diced
1 lb. mushroom, sliced
1/2 tsp chili flakes
1 1/2 tsp dried basil
1 1/2 tsp dried oregano

1 tsp salt
1 tsp pepper
2 bay leaves
1 (28 oz.) cans diced tomatoes
1 (6 oz.) cans tomato paste
2 (10 oz.) cans cream of chicken soup

Directions

1. Prepare the spaghetti by following the instructions on the package. Drain it.
2. Place a pan over medium heat. Cook in it the beef for 8 min. Stir in the garlic, onion, green pepper, celery, mushrooms, and spices.
3. Cook them for 22 min over low heat. Stir in the tomatoes with tomato paste, chicken soup, a pinch of salt and pepper.
4. Let them cook until they start boiling. Lower the heat and let them cook for 22 min.
5. Serve your chili spaghetti warm with some extra spaghetti sauce
6. Enjoy.

LISETTE'S
Pizza

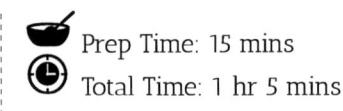

Prep Time: 15 mins
Total Time: 1 hr 5 mins

Servings per Recipe: 8
Calories   451.9
Fat   18.3g
Cholesterol   107.6mg
Sodium   1163.6mg
Carbohydrates   41.1g
Protein   30.6g

Ingredients

8 oz. spaghetti, broken in half
2 eggs
1/2 C. skim milk
3 C. shredded part-skim mozzarella cheese
8 oz. fresh spinach, cooked and chopped
1/2 tsp garlic powder

1 (32 oz.) jars spaghetti sauce, uncooked
Garnish
2 C. cooked broccoli florets
1 medium zucchini, sliced

Directions

1. Before you do anything, preheat the oven to 425 F.
2. Prepare the spaghetti by following the instructions on the package. Drain it.
3. Get a mixing bowl: Whisk in it the eggs. Mix in it the milk with 1 C. of mozzarella cheese, garlic powder and spinach.
4. Add the uncooked spaghetti and combine them well. Pour the mixture into a greased baking dish.
5. Place the casserole in the oven and let it cook for 16 min. Pour over it the spaghetti sauce.
6. Lay the broccoli and zucchini on top followed by the mozzarella cheese.
7. Lower the oven heat to 350 F. Place the casserole in the oven and let it cook for 36 min.
8. Allow the spaghetti casserole to sit for 6 min. Serve it warm.
9. Enjoy.

Vegan Meatballs with Spaghetti

🥣 Prep Time: 15 mins
🕐 Total Time: 45 mins

Servings per Recipe: 1
Calories	82.0
Fat	5.3g
Cholesterol	10.3mg
Sodium	131.1mg
Carbohydrates	4.5g
Protein	4.9g

Ingredients

3 tbsp olive oil
1 large onion, chopped
3 garlic cloves, minced
1 large carrot, grated
1 green pepper, chopped
1 1/2 tsp dried basil
3/4 tsp dried oregano
2 large eggs
1 C. whole wheat breadcrumbs
3/4 C. walnuts, ground

1/4 C. fresh parsley, chopped
1 1/2 tbsp Dijon mustard
1 1/2 tbsp sesame oil
3 tbsp soy sauce
salt and black pepper,
3 lbs. firm tofu, pressed and crumbled

Directions

1. Before you do anything, preheat the oven to 350 F.
2. Place a pan over medium heat. Heat in it the oil. Cook in it the onion, carrot, pepper, garlic and dried herbs for 11 min.
3. Get a mixing bowl: Whisk in it the eggs with bread crumbs, walnuts, parsley, mustard, sesame oil, and soy sauce.
4. Mix in the tofu with cooked veggies. Shape the mixture into 1 1/2 inch meatballs. Place them on a lined up baking tray.
5. Place it in the oven and let it cook for 22 to 28 min.
6. Serve your meatballs warm with some spaghetti sauce and cooked spaghetti.
7. Enjoy.

5-INGRDIENT
Spaghetti

Prep Time: 20 mins
Total Time: 35 mins

Servings per Recipe: 4
Calories	512.6
Fat	21.9g
Cholesterol	94.9mg
Sodium	857.8mg
Carbohydrates	45.3g
Protein	31.2g

Ingredients

1 lb. lean ground beef
0.5 (4 oz.) packages Cream Cheese, cubed
0.5 (8 oz.) packages spaghetti, cooked and drained

1 (24 oz.) jars Italian sauce
2 tbsp grated parmesan cheese

Directions

1. Place a pan over medium heat. Brown in it the beef for 8 min. Discard the fat.
2. Add the Italian sauce with cream cheese, a pinch of salt and pepper. Lower the heat and let them cook for 4 min.
3. Stir in the spaghetti with parmesan cheese. Cook them for 1 to 2 min until the cheese melts.
4. Serve your cream spaghetti warm with some chopped herbs.
5. Enjoy.

Cheesy Garlic Spaghetti

🍲 Prep Time: 10 mins
🕐 Total Time: 25 mins

Servings per Recipe: 1
Calories	1713.5
Fat	92.9g
Cholesterol	186.7mg
Sodium	1283.8mg
Carbohydrates	175.2g
Protein	43.9g

Ingredients

8 oz. spaghetti
4 tbsp butter
2 tbsp olive oil
2 garlic cloves, minced

2 oz. feta cheese
1/8 C. parmesan cheese

Directions

1. Prepare the spaghetti by following the instructions on the package. Drain it.
2. Place a pan over medium heat. Heat in it the butter with oil. Cook in it the garlic for 1 min.
3. Stir in the spaghetti. Sprinkle the parmesan and feta cheese on top. Toss them to coat.
4. Serve your cheesy spaghetti warm.
5. Enjoy.

PESTO
Spaghetti with Chicken Meatballs

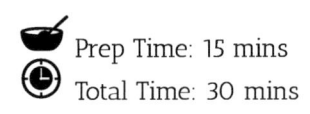 Prep Time: 15 mins
Total Time: 30 mins

Servings per Recipe: 4
Calories	779.5
Fat	30.3g
Cholesterol	182.5mg
Sodium	338.0mg
Carbohydrates	85.6g
Protein	39.4g

Ingredients

Noodles
3/4 lb. spaghetti
2 tbsp olive oil
1 C. chicken stock
1/2 C. cream
1/4 C. Parmigiano-Reggiano cheese, grated
1/4 C. fresh basil, chopped
salt and pepper

Meat
1 lb. ground chicken
1/3 C. store-bought pesto sauce
1/3 C. breadcrumbs
1 egg
1/2 C. flour

Directions

1. Prepare the spaghetti by following the instructions on the package. Drain it. To make the meatballs:
2. Get a mixing bowl: Mix in it the chicken with pesto sauce, breadcrumbs, egg, a pinch of salt and pepper.
3. Shape the mixture into bite size meatballs. Toss them slightly in the flour then place them on a cookie sheet.
4. Place a saucepan over medium heat. Heat in it the oil. Cook in it the meatballs until they become golden brown.
5. Stir in the cream with stock. Cook them until they start boiling. Lower the heat and let them cook for 10 to 16 min or until the meatballs are done.
6. Stir in the basil with parmesan cheese. Stir it until it melts.
7. Place the spaghetti on serving plates. Spoon the meatballs with their sauce on top. Enjoy.

Sage Spaghetti with Potatoes

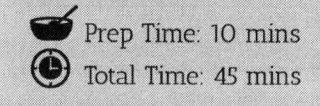

Prep Time: 10 mins
Total Time: 45 mins

Servings per Recipe: 6

Calories	819.2
Fat	6.6g
Cholesterol	14.6mg
Sodium	290.4mg
Carbohydrates	161.5g
Protein	29.1g

Ingredients

8 large potatoes, peeled and sliced
olive oil
1 tsp dried thyme
1 large onion, sliced
4 garlic cloves, chopped
1/2 C. sage leaf
17.5 spaghetti
1 1/2 C. vegetable stock
sea salt

fresh ground black pepper
1 large lemon, juice
3.5oz. parmesan cheese, shaved

Directions

1. Before you do anything, preheat the oven to 400 F.
2. Lay the potato slices on a lined up baking sheet. Toss in it the thyme with a drizzle of olive oil.
3. Place the pan in the oven and let it cook for 16 to 21 min until they become golden brown.
4. Place a saucepan over medium heat. Heat in it 1 tbsp of olive oil. Cook in it the garlic with onion for 3 min.
5. Stir in the sage and cook them for 30 sec. Add the spaghetti and stir them well.
6. Stir in the stock with a pinch of salt and pepper. Let them cook for 2 to 3 min.
7. Remove the potato pan from the oven. Mix in it the potato slices with lemon juice. Bake them for an extra 2 min.
8. Serve your spaghetti warm with the crunchy potato and some bread rolls.
9. Enjoy.

SPAGHETTI
with Broccoli Sauce

Prep Time: 15 mins
Total Time: 30 mins

Servings per Recipe: 4
Calories   855.3
Fat   38.6g
Cholesterol   110.4mg
Sodium   1646.6mg
Carbohydrates   98.5g
Protein   29.8g

Ingredients

1 lb. spaghetti, cooked
24 oz. half-and-half cream
1/4 C. butter
1/2 lb. small broccoli floret
1 C. sliced mushrooms
1/4 C. minced parsley
1 1/2 tsp fresh minced garlic

1 tbsp black pepper
2 tsp salt
3/4 C. grated parmesan cheese

Directions

1. Place a small saucepan over medium heat. cream, butter, broccoli, mushrooms, parsley and seasonings.
2. Cook them for 4 to 6 min. Let them cook until they start boiling. Stir in the spaghetti.
3. Lower the heat and let them cook for 2 to 3 min.
4. Adjust the seasoning of your spaghetti then serve it warm.
5. Enjoy.

Sophomore Year
Spaghetti

🥣 Prep Time: 15 mins
🕐 Total Time: 45 mins

Servings per Recipe: 8
Calories	542.2
Fat	22.8g
Cholesterol	81.6mg
Sodium	1384.8mg
Carbohydrates	56.0g
Protein	27.3g

Ingredients

1 green pepper, diced
1 C. celery, diced
1 medium onion, diced
2 tbsp butter
2 C. cooked chicken, boned
1/4 C. pimiento
1/4-1/2 C. mushroom, sliced canned
1 lb. spaghetti

1 (10 1/2 oz.) cans cream of mushroom soup
1 (10 1/2 oz.) cans cream of chicken soup
1 lb. Velveeta cheese
grated cheddar cheese

Directions

1. Before you do anything, preheat the oven to 350 F.
2. Heat the broth in a large saucepan until it starts boiling. Cook in it the spaghetti for 7 to 8 min until it becomes dente.
3. Before you do anything, preheat the oven to 350 F.
4. Place a pan over medium heat. Heat in it the oil. Cook in it the pepper, celery, and onion in butter for 3 min.
5. Place a small saucepan over medium heat. Combine in it the soups with cheese.
6. Let them cook until the cheese melts. Stir in the spaghetti with cooked veggies, a pinch of salt and pepper.
7. Pour the mixture into a casserole dish. Place it in the oven and let it cook for 32 to 36 min.
8. Serve your spaghetti casserole warm and enjoy.
9. Enjoy.

ARABIAN
Spaghetti

Prep Time: 40 mins
Total Time: 2 hrs 10 mins

Servings per Recipe: 8

Calories	698.4
Fat	38.2g
Cholesterol	121.9mg
Sodium	119.5mg
Carbohydrates	49.5g
Protein	38.2g

Ingredients

1 whole chicken, 3 lb.
2 tbsp extra-virgin olive oil
1 tsp cumin
1/2 tsp allspice
1/4 tsp cayenne pepper
salt & ground black pepper
chicken broth

1/3 C. raisins, soaked in warm water and drained
1/2 C. pine nuts, lightly toasted
1 lb. spaghetti
1/4 C. slivered almonds, toasted
1/4 C. fresh parsley leaves, chopped

Directions

1. Before you do anything, preheat the oven to 350 F. Grease a baking sheet and place it aside. Get a small mixing bowl: Mix in it the oil with cumin, allspice and pepper. Coat the whole chicken with the spice mix. Season it with some salt and pepper. Place it in roasting dish with the breast facing down. Cook it in the oven for 1 h.
2. Flip the chicken and let it cook for an extra 35 min. Allow it to cool down for a while.
3. Shred the chicken and reserve the meat.
4. Place a large saucepan over medium heat. Pour in it all the chicken juice from the pan and add more water to make 1 C. of it.
5. Stir in the raisins and the pine nuts, a pinch of salt and pepper. Cook them until they start simmering.
6. Lower the heat and let them cook until the sauce reduces and becomes slightly thick.
7. Prepare the pasta by following the instructions on the package. Drain it. Add the pasta with shredded chicken to the raisins sauce. Toss them to coat. Serve your pasta warm. Garnish it with parsley and almonds.
8. Enjoy.

Spaghetti
Merlot Drums

🥘 Prep Time: 5 mins
🕐 Total Time: 2 hrs 5 mins

Servings per Recipe: 4
Calories	665.0
Fat	36.0g
Cholesterol	242.5mg
Sodium	989.1mg
Carbohydrates	25.6g
Protein	56.2g

Ingredients

7 chicken legs
1 (28 oz.) cans crushed tomatoes
1 (8 oz.) cans tomato sauce
1/4 C. merlot
1 large onion, diced
2 garlic cloves, minced
1 tsp basil
1/2 tsp oregano

salt and pepper
celery salt
3 carrots, peeled and diced
olive oil

Directions

1. Season the chicken legs with some salt and pepper.
2. Place a large pot over medium heat. Heat in it the oil. Cook in it the chicken legs until they become golden brown.
3. Drain the chicken legs and discard their skin. Stir them back into the pot with garlic, and onion. Cook them for 3 to 4 min.
4. Stir in the merlot and cook them for 2 to 3 min. Stir in the carrots and cook them until the wine becomes thick.
5. Stir in the tomato with spices and tomato sauce. Lower the heat and let them cook for 120 min.
6. Once the time is up, serve your chicken legs stew with some spaghetti.
7. Enjoy.

TUESDAY'S
Dinner (Lemon Pasta with Chicken Cutlets)

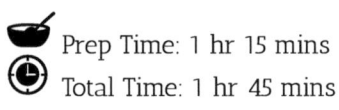

Prep Time: 1 hr 15 mins
Total Time: 1 hr 45 mins

Servings per Recipe: 5
Calories	435.2
Fat	20.4g
Cholesterol	58.1mg
Sodium	526.8mg
Carbohydrates	34.4g
Protein	28.4g

Ingredients

1 lb. chicken breast, cut into pieces
3 lemons, juice
4 tbsp oil
1 tsp minced onion, dried
1 tsp minced garlic
1/2 tsp black pepper
1/2 tsp oregano

1 tsp salt
8 oz. thin spaghetti

Directions

1. Get a mixing bowl: Whisk in it the lemon juice with salt, oregano, garlic, onion, and oil.
2. Get a zip lock bag: Place in it the chicken and with the lemon mixture. Seal the bag and shake it to coat.
3. Let it sit for 60 min in the fridge.
4. Before you do anything, preheat the oven to 350 F.
5. Pour the chicken with the marinade into a greased baking dish. Place it in the oven and let it cook for 32 min.
6. Prepare the spaghetti by following the instructions on the package. Drain it.
7. Spoon the baked lemon chicken over the spaghetti then serve it warm
8. Enjoy.

Arizona Spaghetti

🥄 Prep Time: 15 mins
🕐 Total Time: 45 mins

Servings per Recipe: 6	
Calories	238.6
Fat	5.5g
Cholesterol	12.0mg
Sodium	669.8mg
Carbohydrates	37.9g
Protein	10.1g

Ingredients

1 1/4 lbs. turkey bratwursts, ground
1 C. onion, chopped
2 tsp garlic, minced
2 tsp chili powder
1 tsp ground cumin
1 (14 1/2 oz.) cans Rotel Tomatoes, chili seasoned
3/4 C. picante sauce

1 tsp dried oregano
1 C. cheese, shredded
8 oz. spaghetti, cooked and drained

Directions

1. Place a pan over medium heat. Cook in it the crumbled sausages.
2. Stir in the onion, garlic, chili powder, and cumin for 9 min.
3. Stir in the tomatoes, picante sauce, oregano, a pinch of salt and pepper. Cook them until they start boiling.
4. Lower the heat and let the sauce cook for 18 to 22 min.
5. Place the spaghetti in serving bowl. Spoon the hot sauce over it.
6. Garnish it with shredded cheese then serve it right away.
7. Enjoy.

SPAGHETTI
Garden Party

Prep Time: 20 mins
Total Time: 35 mins

Servings per Recipe: 5
Calories	535.7
Fat	17.2g
Cholesterol	2.6mg
Sodium	348.2mg
Carbohydrates	80.6g
Protein	15.6g

Ingredients

1 lb. spaghetti
2 tomatoes, diced
1 green pepper, seeded and diced
1 red pepper, seeded and diced
2 zucchini, diced
3 celery ribs, sliced
2 carrots, sliced
6 oz. sliced black olives, drained

1/4 C. olive oil
3 tbsp parmesan cheese
2 tsp minced garlic
1 tsp basil
salt and pepper
shredded mozzarella cheese
1 1/2 C. cooked chicken, chopped

Directions

1. Prepare the spaghetti by following the instructions on the package. Drain it.
2. Place a large pan over medium heat. Heat in it the oil. Cook in it the veggies for 6 to 10 min until it become soft.
3. Get a small mixing bowl: Whisk in it the oil, cheese, garlic, basil, salt and pepper to make the dressing.
4. Get a large mixing bowl: Toss in it the veggies with dressing. Spoon the mixture over the spaghetti.
5. Garnish your salad with some mozzarella cheese then serve it.
6. Enjoy.

Spaghetti
Japanese House Style

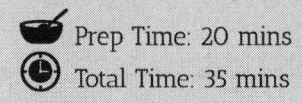
Prep Time: 20 mins
Total Time: 35 mins

Servings per Recipe: 3	
Calories	388.8
Fat	4.7g
Cholesterol	47.8mg
Sodium	1337.6mg
Carbohydrates	73.8g
Protein	15.7g

Ingredients

1 small onion, chopped
1 sweet red pepper, sliced
4 medium mushrooms, sliced
1/2 head bok choy, sliced
1/2 C. green peas, frozen
1/2 C. bean sprouts
1 (6 oz.) cans water chestnuts, drained & rinsed

1 tsp sesame oil
2 tbsp Worcestershire sauce
2 tbsp ketchup
2 tbsp light soy sauce
2 tbsp oyster sauce
6 oz. Japanese noodles

Directions

1. Before you do anything, preheat the oven to 450 F. Grease a baking sheet and place it aside.
2. Get a mixing bowl: Whisk in it the ketchup with soy, Worcestershire, and oyster sauces.
3. Prepare the spaghetti by following the instructions on the package. Drain it.
4. Place a pan over medium heat. Heat in it the oil. Cook in it the peppers, mushroom, garlic, onion, bean sprouts, and peas for 6 min.
5. Stir in the chestnuts, and bok choy. Cook them for 4 min. Stir in the noodles with ketchup sauce.
6. Adjust the seasoning of your stir fry then serve it.
7. Enjoy.

HONOLULU
Pineapple Spaghetti

🥣 Prep Time: 20 mins
🕐 Total Time: 1 hr 5 mins

Servings per Recipe: 4
Calories	903.9
Fat	22.2g
Cholesterol	85.0mg
Sodium	3095.1mg
Carbohydrates	121.6g
Protein	56.1g

Ingredients

1 lb. hamburger
4 (10 1/2 oz.) cans beef gravy
1/3 C. soy sauce
1 medium onion
1 medium green pepper
1 lb. spaghetti

2 (8 oz.) cans mushrooms, drained
2 tbsp sugar
1 (6 oz.) cans pineapple chunks, drained

Directions

1. Before you do anything, preheat the oven to 350 F.
2. Cook the spaghetti by following the instructions on the package for 5 min only. Drain it.
3. Place a large pan over medium heat. Cook in it the meat with onion, mushroom and green pepper.
4. Cook them for 8 min while stirring them often. Stir in the sugar. Discard the fat.
5. Get a mixing bowl: Whisk in it the soy sauce with gravy. Stir into the meat sauce with spaghetti and pineapple, a pinch of salt and pepper.
6. Pour the mixture into a baking dish. Place it in the oven and let it cook for 35 to 46 min.
7. Serve your spaghetti dish warm.
8. Enjoy.

Spaghetti with Eggplant Sauce

🥄 Prep Time: 15 mins

🕐 Total Time: 1 hr 30 mins

Servings per Recipe: 6	
Calories	518.7
Fat	13.4g
Cholesterol	0.0mg
Sodium	298.2mg
Carbohydrates	86.0g
Protein	15.4g

Ingredients

17.5 oz. aubergines, diced
salt
olive oil
4 tbsp extra virgin olive oil
4 garlic cloves, chopped
2 small dried red chilies, crumbled
1 C. black olives, stoned and chopped
2 tbsp capers
1 kg large fresh tomatoes, skinned and chopped

2 tbsp tomato puree
2 tsp dried Italian seasoning
salt & ground black pepper
500 g spaghetti
fresh basil leaf
grated parmesan cheese

Directions

1. Cook the spaghetti by following the instructions on the package. Drain it.
2. Season the eggplant dices with some salt. Let them sit for 18 minutes.
3. Discard the excess water and dry them.
4. Place a pan over medium heat. Heat in it a splash of oil. Cook in it the eggplant dices until they become golden brown.
5. Drain them and place them aside. Stir in the garlic with chili flakes. Cook them for 45 seconds.
6. Stir in the olives, capers, tomatoes, puree and dried seasoning. Put on the lid and let them cook for 32 to 36 min over low heat.
7. Stir in the cooked eggplant dices with spaghetti and basil leaves.
8. Adjust the seasoning of your spaghetti then serve it warm with some grated parmesan cheese.
9. Get a mixing bowl:
10. Enjoy.

CANCUN
Spaghetti

🍳 Prep Time: 20 mins
🕐 Total Time: 2 hrs 20 mins

Servings per Recipe: 4
Calories	763.3
Fat	20.2g
Cholesterol	77.1mg
Sodium	1666.5mg
Carbohydrates	105.2g
Protein	42.5g

Ingredients

1 lb. ground beef
1 medium onion, chopped
1 green bell pepper, chopped
2 garlic cloves, minced
1 (29 oz.) cans tomato puree
1 (15 1/2 oz.) cans kidney beans, drained
1 C. water

2 tbsp chili powder
1 tsp cumin
1 tsp oregano
2 tsp salt
1/4-1/2 tsp cayenne pepper
12 oz. spaghetti

Directions

1. Cook the spaghetti by following the instructions on the package for 5 min only. Drain it.
2. Place a pan over medium heat. Cook in it the beef with garlic and bell peppers for 10 min. Discard the fat.
3. Stir in the beans with spices and tomato purée. Put on the lid and let them cook for 120 min over low heat.
4. When the sauce becomes thick, turn off the heat.
5. Place the spaghetti on serving plates. Spoon the sauce over it with some grated cheese.
6. Enjoy.

Italian
Puttanesca Pasta

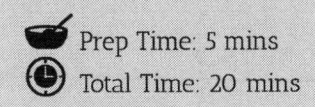 Prep Time: 5 mins
Total Time: 20 mins

Servings per Recipe: 4
Calories	546.3
Fat	10.8g
Cholesterol	0.0mg
Sodium	334.3mg
Carbohydrates	95.6g
Protein	17.2g

Ingredients

4 garlic cloves, minced
salt
1 lb. spaghetti
2 tbsp olive oil
1 tsp red pepper flakes
4 tsp minced anchovies
1 (28 oz.) cans diced tomatoes, drained,
juice reserved

3 tbsp capers, rinsed
1/2 C. black olives, pitted and chopped
1/4 C. minced fresh parsley leaves

Directions

1. Get a small mixing bowl: Stir in it 1 tbsp of water with garlic.
2. Place a large pot over medium heat. Heat in it 4 quarts of water. Add it the pasta with 1 tbsp of salt.
3. Let it cook for 8 to 10 min or until it is done. Drain it. Toss it with 1/4 C. of tomato juice.
4. Place a large pan over medium heat. Stir in it the garlic and water mix with oil, red pepper flakes and anchovies for 1 min.
5. Add the tomato and let them cook for 9 min over low heat to make the sauce.
6. Add the capers, olives, parsley, a pinch of salt and pepper. Cook them for 1 to 2 min
7. Place the spaghetti on serving plates. Spoon over it the tomato sauce then serve it hot.
8. Enjoy.

5-INGREDIENT
Spaghetti

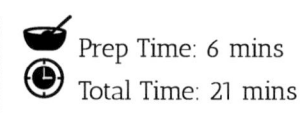

Prep Time: 6 mins
Total Time: 21 mins

Servings per Recipe: 4
Calories	610.3
Fat	8.9g
Cholesterol	0.0mg
Sodium	10.8mg
Carbohydrates	111.5g
Protein	19.1g

Ingredients

17.5 oz. spaghetti
2 onions
2 tbsp olive oil

salt
white pepper

Directions

1. Follow the instructions on the package to cook the spaghetti. Drain it.
2. Place a large pan over medium heat. Heat in it the oil. Cook in it the onion for 3 to 4 min.
3. Stir in the spaghetti with a pinch of salt and pepper. Serve it warm.
4. Enjoy.

Spaghetti
Squashed

Prep Time: 10 mins
Total Time: 40 mins

Servings per Recipe: 6
Calories	156.2
Fat	10.3g
Cholesterol	0.0mg
Sodium	39.4mg
Carbohydrates	17.1g
Protein	1.6g

Ingredients

3 lbs. spaghetti squash, halved, seeds and fiber removed
1/4 C. olive oil
1 tbsp fresh rosemary, chopped
3 garlic cloves, fresh minced
1/2 onion, sliced

parmesan cheese, grated
black pepper, fresh ground
nutmeg, fresh grated
salt

Directions

1. Slice the squash in half. Place it in a baking dish with its cut up sides facing down.
2. Place the pan in the microwave and cook it for 20 min on high.
3. Place a large skillet over medium heat. Heat in it 2 tbsp of oil. Cook in it the garlic with onion for 6 min.
4. Stir in the rosemary an cook them for 3 min.
5. Use a fork to scrap the squash pulp then stir it into the pan with a pinch of salt and pepper.
6. Sprinkle the cheese with a pinch of nutmeg on top. Serve it warm.
7. Enjoy.

MARIA'S
Alla-Mamma Pasta

Prep Time: 15 mins
Total Time: 35 mins

Servings per Recipe: 4	
Calories	438.2
Fat	10.4g
Cholesterol	116.6mg
Sodium	1048.6mg
Carbohydrates	59.0g
Protein	26.3g

Ingredients

10 oz. spaghetti
2 C. parsley, chopped
7 oz. shrimp
2 oz. anchovies, chopped
1 tbsp tomato paste
1 C. tomatoes, canned
2 tbsp pepperoni, chopped
1 tbsp garlic, minced

2 tbsp olive oil
salt
pepper

Directions

1. Prepare the pasta by following the instructions on the package.
2. Place a pan over medium heat. Heat in it the oil. Cook in it the parsley with anchovies, garlic, pepperoni, and shrimps for 2 min.
3. Stir in the tomato paste and cook them for 40 seconds. Stir in the canned tomato and cook them for 3 min.
4. Toss the spaghetti with the shrimp sauce, a pinch of salt and pepper. Serve it hot.
5. Enjoy.

Amish
Friendship Omelets

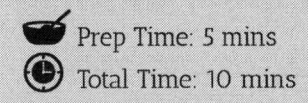 Prep Time: 5 mins
Total Time: 10 mins

Servings per Recipe: 2

Calories	933.8
Fat	52.5g
Cholesterol	372.0mg
Sodium	152.5mg
Carbohydrates	78.9g
Protein	35.4g

Ingredients

salt
1/2 lb. thin spaghetti
6 tbsp extra virgin olive oil
2 large garlic cloves, lightly smashed and peeled
4 eggs

fresh ground black pepper
grated parmesan cheese

Directions

1. Prepare the pasta by following the instructions on the package. Drain it.
2. Place a saucepan over medium heat. Heat in it 4 tbsp of oil. Sauté in it the garlic for 1 min.
3. Drain the garlic and place it aside. Stir the rest of the oil into the pan. Cook in it the eggs to your liking.
4. Use a fork to break the fried egg into pieces with garlic.
5. Add the spaghetti with a pinch of salt and pepper. Toss them to coat.
6. Serve your spaghetti hot right away.
7. Enjoy.

PECORINO
Romano
Spaghetti

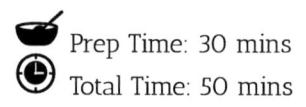 Prep Time: 30 mins

Total Time: 50 mins

Servings per Recipe: 4
Calories	553.9
Fat	3.3g
Cholesterol	2.8mg
Sodium	77.0mg
Carbohydrates	108.7g
Protein	20.4g

Ingredients

1 1/4 lbs. spaghetti
3/4 C. pecorino Romano cheese, grated
1/4 C. Parmigiano-Reggiano cheese, grated

2 tbsp ground black pepper
kosher salt

Directions

1. Prepare the pasta by following the instructions on the package until it becomes dente for about 7 min.
2. Drain it. Place 1/2 C. of the cooking liquid aside.
3. Place a saucepan over medium heat. Combine in it the spaghetti with reserved water, and cheese.
4. Season them with some salt and pepper then toss them to coat. Serve it warm.
5. Enjoy.

Pennsylvania Sunset Herbed Glazed Spaghetti

Prep Time: 10 mins
Total Time: 40 mins

Servings per Recipe: 6
Calories   412.1
Fat   4.9 g
Cholesterol   115.2 mg
Sodium   120.8 mg
Carbohydrates   64.1 g
Protein   26.5 g

Ingredients

1 lb. large shrimp, clean and divined
10 garlic cloves, peeled and minced
3 tsp olive oil
2 C. vegetable broth
2 tomatoes, sliced
1 onion, chopped
1 capsicum, chopped
2 tsp dried basil

2 tsp dried tarragon
2 tsp dried oregano
1 dash pepper
1 dash chili
1 lb. pasta, cooked

Directions

1. Place a pan over medium heat. Heat in it the oil. Cook in it the garlic for 4 min.
2. Stir in the broth and let them cook for 16 min. Stir in the tomatoes, onion, capsicum and herbs.
3. Let them cook for 7 min. Stir in the shrimp and let them cook for 3 to 5 min until it becomes pink.
4. Stir the pasta into the sauce then season it with some salt and pepper.
5. Serve your spaghetti hot with some grated cheese.
6. Enjoy.

BACKROAD
Oven Beef and Spaghetti Casserole

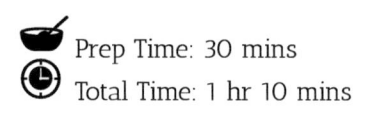 Prep Time: 30 mins
Total Time: 1 hr 10 mins

Servings per Recipe: 4
Calories	496.5
Fat	19.4g
Cholesterol	71.1mg
Sodium	694.3mg
Carbohydrates	54.6g
Protein	28.3g

Ingredients

1/2 lb. spaghetti, broken into pieces
1 lb. ground beef
1 medium onion, chopped
2 - 3 minced garlic cloves
1 small green bell pepper, chopped
1/2 lb. fresh mushrooms, sliced
seasoning salt
pepper

3 tbsp grated parmesan cheese
1 - 2 tsp chili powder
1 tbsp Worcestershire sauce
1 (14 oz.) cans tomatoes
1 (14 oz.) cans canned corn niblets
1 C. grated cheddar cheese
1 (10 1/2 oz.) cans tomato soup

Directions

1. Prepare the pasta by following the instructions on the package. Drain it.
2. Place a large pan over medium heat. Cook in it the ground beef with onion, garlic, green pepper and mushrooms for 8 to 10 min.
3. Discard the fat. Stir in the cheese with chili powder, tomato, corn, tomato soup and Worcestershire sauce.
4. Let them cook for 42 to 46 min. Spoon the sauce over the cooked spaghetti.
5. Garnish it with some extra cheese then serve it hot.
6. Enjoy.

Hermosa Ranch
Pasta Salad

Prep Time: 35 mins
Total Time: 55 mins

Servings per Recipe: 4
Calories   842.4
Fat   52.7g
Cholesterol   261.0mg
Sodium   1397.4mg
Carbohydrates   65.3g
Protein   30.0g

Ingredients

2 C. uncooked seashell pasta noodles
3 eggs, hard boiled and peeled
1 (3 oz.) packages pepperoni, sliced
1 (8 oz.) packages cheddar cheese, shredded
1 medium size zucchini, chopped
2 - 3 bunches green onions, sliced
Dressing
2 tbsp dry hidden valley ranch dressing mix
1/3 C. milk

1 C. mayonnaise
2 tsp mustard
1/2 tsp sugar
1/4 tsp celery seed
1/4 tsp salt
1/8 tsp pepper
1/8 tsp oregano

Directions

1. Prepare the noodles by following the instructions on the package. Drain it.
2. Get a mixing bowl: Whisk in it the ranch dressing with milk, mayo, sugar, celery seed, oregano, salt and pepper.
3. Get a mixing bowl: Toss in it the noodles with chopped eggs and dressing.
4. Place the salad in the fridge for at least 1 h then serve it.
5. Enjoy.

HERBED
Spaghetti

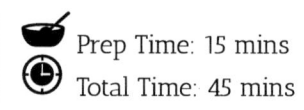

Prep Time: 15 mins
Total Time: 45 mins

Servings per Recipe: 4
Calories	288.6
Fat	5.0g
Cholesterol	0.0mg
Sodium	6.9mg
Carbohydrates	51.6g
Protein	9.6g

Ingredients

2 - 4 garlic cloves, peeled and minced
3 tsp olive oil
2 C. vegetable broth
2 tomatoes, chopped
1 onion, chopped
1 red capsicums
2 tsp dried basil
2 tsp dried tarragon
2 tsp dried oregano
black pepper,
ground red chili pepper,
4 C. cooked spaghetti

Directions

1. Place a pan over medium heat. Heat in it the oil. Cook in it the garlic for 3 to 4 min.
2. Stir in the broth and let them cook for 16 min over low heat.
3. Stir in the tomatoes, onion, bell pepper and herbs. Let them cook for 12 min.
4. Spoon the sauce over the spaghetti then serve it hot.
5. Enjoy.

Mexican
Spaghetti with Corn Casserole

Prep Time: 10 mins
Total Time: 1 hr 10 mins

Servings per Recipe: 4
Calories	697.9
Fat	29.0g
Cholesterol	67.8mg
Sodium	1121.9mg
Carbohydrates	86.7g
Protein	28.4g

Ingredients

8 oz. spaghetti, broken into 4 parts
2 C. mild cheddar cheese, shredded
1 (15 1/4 oz.) cans cream-style corn
1 (15 1/4 oz.) cans whole kernel corn, drained

2 tbsp margarine, melted
1 C. milk

Directions

1. Before you do anything, preheat the oven to 350 F.
2. Stir corn with milk and 1 1/2 C. of cheese in a baking dish.
3. Stir in the spaghetti and push it down to cover it with the mix. Top it with cheese.
4. Drizzle the melted margarine on top. Lay a loose sheet of oil on top to cover it.
5. Place the dish in the oven and let it cook for 60 min. Serve it hot.
6. Enjoy.

COUNTRY
Spaghetti Squash Casserole

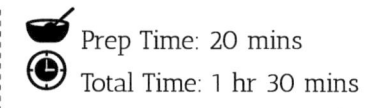

Prep Time: 20 mins
Total Time: 1 hr 30 mins

Servings per Recipe: 4

Calories	507.4
Fat	32.2g
Cholesterol	139.3mg
Sodium	636.6mg
Carbohydrates	13.4g
Protein	41.3g

Ingredients

1 spaghetti squash, halved and seeded
1 lb. chicken breast, cubed
1/2 C. diced green bell pepper
1/2 C. diced red bell pepper
1/4 C. diced red onion
1 garlic clove, chopped
1 (14 1/2 oz.) cans can Italian-style
diced tomatoes, drained

1/2 tsp dried oregano
1/2 tsp dried basil
1/4 tsp salt
2 1/4 C. shredded cheddar cheese

Directions

1. Before you do anything, preheat the oven to 375 F.
2. Slice the squash in half and place on a baking tray with the cut up side facing down.
3. Place it in the oven and let it cook for 45 to 60 min until it becomes soft. Place it aside to cool down then shred it.
4. Lower the oven heat to 350 F.
5. Place a pan over medium heat. Heat in it a splash of oil. Cook in it the chicken, peppers, onion and garlic for 8 to 10 min.
6. Stir in the spaghetti squash with tomato and spices. Let them cook for 4 to 5 min. Turn off the heat and stir in 2 C. of cheese until it melts. Pour the mixture into a greased baking dish.
7. Place it in the oven and let it cook for 26 min. Top it with the remaining cheese.
8. Allow the spaghetti casserole to sit for few minutes then serve it warm. Enjoy.

Twin Cities
Spaghetti
Hamburgers

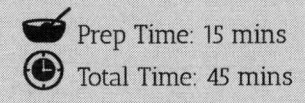 Prep Time: 15 mins

Total Time: 45 mins

Servings per Recipe: 2

Calories	1254.3
Fat	55.3g
Cholesterol	205.4mg
Sodium	1990.3mg
Carbohydrates	121.6g
Protein	67.5g

Ingredients

1/2 lb. spaghetti, broken into 3 parts
1 lb. ground beef
2 tbsp tomato ketchup
1 (1 1/4 oz.) packages onion soup mix
2 tbsp butter
1 medium onion, chopped

1/3 C. celery, chopped
1 (28 oz.) cans tomatoes
1/2 tsp celery salt
1/3 C. cheddar cheese, grated

Directions

1. Before you do anything, preheat the oven to 350 F.
2. Prepare the noodles by following the instructions on the package. Drain it.
3. Get a mixing bowl: Mix in it the beef, Ketchup, onion soup, a pinch of salt and pepper.
4. Form the mixture into burgers
5. Place a pan over medium heat. Melt in it the butter. Cook in it the burgers for 4 to 5 min on each side.
6. Drain them and place them aside. Stir the onion with celery into the same pan. Cook them for 3 min.
7. Stir in the tomato with spines. Cook them until they start boiling. Let them cook for an extra 6 min.
8. Add the pasta and toss them to coat. Pour the mixture into a greased baking dish.
9. Lay the beef burgers on top followed by cheese. Place the dish in the oven and let it cook for 22 min.
10. Serve it hot.
11. Enjoy.

SPAGHETTI
Squash Lasagna

🥣 Prep Time: 30 mins
🕐 Total Time: 1 hr 30 mins

Servings per Recipe: 6
Calories	386.3
Fat	22.9g
Cholesterol	81.5mg
Sodium	1262.3mg
Carbohydrates	20.6g
Protein	28.0g

Ingredients

1 medium spaghetti squash, halved lengthwise & seeded
1 lb. lean ground turkey
1 onion, chopped
2 tbsp minced garlic cloves
2 (14 oz.) cans stewed tomatoes
1 tbsp dried basil
1 vegetable bouillon cube

black pepper
1 (15 oz.) cans black olives, chopped
1 C. mozzarella cheese, shredded
1 C. parmesan cheese, shredded

Directions

1. Before you do anything, preheat the oven to 325 F.
2. Slice the squash in half and place on a baking tray with the cut up side facing down.
3. Place it in the oven and let it cook for 35 to 400 min until it becomes soft. Place it aside to cool down then shred it.
4. Place a saucepan over medium heat. Grease it with a cooking spray.
5. Cook in it the garlic with onion and turkey for 6 min. Discard the fat.
6. Add the tomatoes, basil, bouillon and pepper. Let them cook for 16 min.
7. Spread half of the spaghetti squash in the bottom of a greased casserole dish.
8. Top it with half of the turkey sauce, half of the olives and half of the mozzarella.
9. Repeat the process to make another layer. Sprinkle the parmesan cheese on top. Cook it in the oven for 22 min.
10. Serve your spaghetti casserole warm.
11. Enjoy.

Creamy
Spaghetti with Yogurt Sauce

Prep Time: 5 mins
Total Time: 25 mins

Servings per Recipe: 4
Calories   668.5
Fat   22.0g
Cholesterol   57.7mg
Sodium   464.0mg
Carbohydrates   98.2g
Protein   19.0g

Ingredients

1 lb. pasta
6 tbsp butter
3 onions, grated
1/2 tsp salt
2 - 3 garlic cloves, minced

1 1/2 C. yogurt, room temperature
ground pepper
fresh herb

Directions

1. Prepare the spaghetti by following the instructions on the package. Drain it.
2. Place a pan over medium heat. Heat in it 4 tbsp of butter.
3. Cook in it the onion with a pinch of salt for 5 to 7 min until it becomes golden brown.
4. Stir in the garlic and cook them for 3 min. Turn off the heat and stir in the rest of the butter.
5. Get a mixing bowl: Toss in it the spaghetti with onion mixture, yogurt, a pinch of salt and pepper.
6. Serve your spaghetti right away with some chopped herbs of your choice.
7. Enjoy.

PASTA NOODLE
Alternative (How to Make Spaghetti Squash)

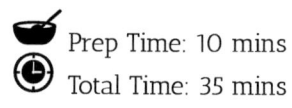

Prep Time: 10 mins
Total Time: 35 mins

Servings per Recipe: 4
Calories   50.9
Fat   5.7g
Cholesterol   15.2mg
Sodium   632.0mg
Carbohydrates   0.0g
Protein   0.0g

Ingredients

1 whole spaghetti squash
2 tbsp butter
1 tsp salt

Directions

1. Use a fork to knife to pierce the squash several times. Place it in the microwave and cook it for 18 min on 70 %.
2. Place the squash aside and let it cool down for few minutes. Slice it in half, discard the seeds and shred it with a fork.
3. Get a mixing bowl: Toss in it the spaghetti squash with butter and a pinch of salt.
4. Serve it with your favorite toppings.
5. Enjoy.

Spaghetti Houston

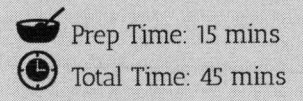
Prep Time: 15 mins
Total Time: 45 mins

Servings per Recipe: 6
Calories	929.2
Fat	42.2g
Cholesterol	208.7mg
Sodium	1980.6mg
Carbohydrates	80.7g
Protein	56.0g

Ingredients

2 lbs. ground sirloin
1 onion, chopped
2 (10 3/4 oz.) cans tomato soup,
1 green pepper, chopped
1 (16 oz.) packages egg noodles, cooked
and drained
2 C. mozzarella cheese

2 (10 3/4 oz.) cans condensed golden
mushroom soup
1 (2 1/4 oz.) cans sliced black olives
1/2 C. parmesan cheese

Directions

1. Before you do anything, preheat the oven to 350 F.
2. Place a pan over medium heat. Cook in it the ground sirloin with onion for 10 min. Discard the fat.
3. Stir in the tomato soup, green pepper and noodles. Put on the lid and let it cook for 12 min over low heat.
4. Pour half of the mix into a greased baking dish. Top it with half of the mozzarella cheese, golden mushroom soup and black olives.
5. Repeat the process to make another layer. Sprinkle the parmesan cheese on top.
6. Place the dish in the oven and let it cook for 32 min. Serve it hot.
7. Enjoy.

PROSCIUTTO
Asparagus Spaghetti Pan

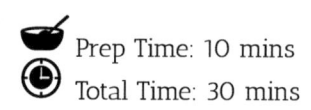 Prep Time: 10 mins

Total Time: 30 mins

Servings per Recipe: 6
Calories	413.1
Fat	16.5g
Cholesterol	22.4mg
Sodium	202.5mg
Carbohydrates	50.1g
Protein	17.5g

Ingredients

2 lbs. asparagus, trimmed
3/4 lb. spaghetti
4 tbsp olive oil
4 cloves garlic, minced
6 oz. prosciutto, strips
6 oz. smoked mozzarella cheese, diced

6 tbsp sliced fresh basil leaves
salt
fresh ground black pepper

Directions

1. Place a pot of water over high heat. Bring it to a boil. Cook in it the asparagus for 3 min.
2. Drain it and place it in some icy water. Let it sit for few minutes. Drain it and cut into 1 inch pieces.
3. Prepare the spaghetti by following the instructions on the package. Cook it for 8 min. Drain it.
4. Reserve 1 C. of the pasta water.
5. Place a large skillet over medium heat. Heat in it the oil. Cook in it the garlic for 1 min.
6. Stir in the prosciutto and cook them for 2 to 3 min.
7. Stir in the reserved pasta water with the cooked pasta, a pinch of salt and pepper.
8. Cook them for 1 to 2 min. Stir in the basil with mozzarella cheese. Stir them to coat.
9. Serve it hot.
10. Enjoy.

Moroccan Pasta with Hummus Sauce

🥄 Prep Time: 5 mins
🕐 Total Time: 20 mins

Servings per Recipe: 4

Calories	426.6
Fat	2.8g
Cholesterol	0.0mg
Sodium	279.1mg
Carbohydrates	89.5g
Protein	18.4g

Ingredients

- 11 oz. whole wheat spaghetti
- 1 red onion, chopped
- 3 garlic cloves, crushed
- 1 C. mushroom, sliced
- 28 oz. chopped tomatoes
- 2 tsp cinnamon
- 2 tsp ground cumin
- 1 tsp turmeric
- 1 pinch salt
- 1 pinch black pepper
- 10 oz. chickpeas, from a can, drained and rinsed
- 3/4 C. fresh parsley, chopped
- 3/4 C. fresh cilantro, chopped

Directions

1. Prepare the spaghetti by following the instructions on the package. Drain it.
2. Place a pan over medium heat. Heat in it a splash of oil. Cook in it the onions, garlic and mushrooms for 6 min.
3. Stir in the tomatoes, cinnamon, cumin, turmeric and salt and pepper. Cook them for 9 min over low medium heat.
4. Add the chickpeas and cook them for 4 min. Add the slices with parsley and cilantro. Cook them for 3 to 4 min.
5. Stir in the spaghetti and toss them to coat.
6. Serve your chickpea spaghetti hot with your favorite toppings.
7. Enjoy.

ITALIAN
Parmesa-Getti Bread

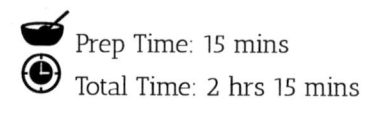

Prep Time: 15 mins
Total Time: 2 hrs 15 mins

Servings per Recipe: 10
Calories	170.3
Fat	2.7g
Cholesterol	2.9mg
Sodium	52.8mg
Carbohydrates	30.3g
Protein	5.5g

Ingredients

2 1/4 tsp yeast
1 1/2 C. water
1 tbsp sugar
1 tsp garlic salt
1/3 C. parmesan cheese, grated
1 tsp dried Italian seasoning

1 tbsp olive oil
3 C. bread flour

Directions

1. Before you do anything, preheat the oven to 350 F. Grease a baking sheet.
2. Get a mixing bowl: Stir in it the warm water with yeast. Let them sit for 8 min.
3. Mix in the sugar, salt, cheese, seasoning, oil and flour. Combine them until you get a smooth dough.
4. Place the dough on a floured surface. Knead it until it becomes soft. Place it in a greased bowl and cover it.
5. Let it sit until it rise and doubles in size. Shape into a loaf and place it on the greased sheet.
6. Before you do anything, preheat the oven to 350 F. Grease a baking sheet.
7. Lay a towel over it to cover it. Let it rest until it rise and doubles in size.
8. Place it in the oven and let it cook for 36 to 42 min. Allow it to cool down completely then serve it.
9. Enjoy.

Spaghetti with Béchamel Sauce

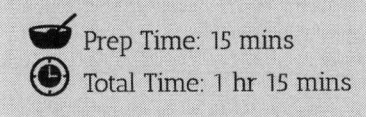

Prep Time: 15 mins
Total Time: 1 hr 15 mins

Servings per Recipe: 4

Calories	860.7
Fat	40.3g
Cholesterol	145.1mg
Sodium	452.6mg
Carbohydrates	79.4g
Protein	44.4g

Ingredients

250 g spaghetti
1 onion
500 g ground beef
1 (410 g) cans tomato puree
1/4 tsp cinnamon
1 bay leaf

salt, pepper
1/2 C. grated parmesan cheese
60 g butter
1/3 C. flour
2 C. milk

Directions

1. Prepare the spaghetti by following the instructions on the package. Drain it. To make the sauce:
2. Place a heavy saucepan over medium heat. Melt in it the butter. mix in the flour and cook it for 1 min.
3. Add the milk gradually while whisking them all the time to make the sauce. Let it cook until the sauce becomes thick.
4. To make the spaghetti sauce: Place a pan over medium heat. Cook in it the onion with beef for 6 min. Discard the fat.
5. Stir in the tomato puree, cinnamon, bay leaf and salt and pepper. Cook it until it starts boiling.
6. Put on the lid and lower the heat. Let it cook for 16 min. Drain and discard the bay leaf.
7. Lay half of the spaghetti in the bottom of a baking dish. Spread over it half of the beef sauce.
8. Repeat the process to make another layer. Drizzle the milk sauce on top followed by cheese.
9. Place the spaghetti dish in the oven. Cook it for 3 min.
10. Serve it hot.
11. Enjoy.

SPAGHETTI
and Cheese Cups

Prep Time: 5 mins
Total Time: 20 mins

Servings per Recipe: 1
Calories	70.5
Fat	5.0g
Cholesterol	71.0mg
Sodium	160.1mg
Carbohydrates	1.3g
Protein	4.8g

Ingredients

14 oz. cans spaghetti in tomato sauce
1 1/2 C. grated cheese
4 eggs, lightly beaten

salt and pepper

Directions

1. Before you do anything, preheat the oven to 350 F. Grease a muffin pan.
2. Get a mixing bowl: Whisk in it the eggs with cheese, a pinch of salt and pepper.
3. Stir in the spaghetti. Divide the mixture between the muffin cups.
4. Place the pan in the oven and let them cook for 16 min.
5. Allow the spaghetti muffins to cool down completely.
6. Enjoy.

Parisian
Spaghetti with Escargot Sauce

Prep Time: 35 mins

Total Time: 55 mins

Servings per Recipe: 4	
Calories	924.5
Fat	53.1g
Cholesterol	138.1mg
Sodium	626.4mg
Carbohydrates	77.8g
Protein	36.1g

Ingredients

12 -16 oz. spaghetti
5 tbsp olive oil
1 sweet onion, chopped
1/2 lb. mushroom, cleaned and stalks trimmed*
4 anchovy fillets, drained and chopped
1 tbsp garlic, chopped
2 tsp cornstarch
2 tbsp lemon juice, squeezed
1 C. crème fraiche

14 oz. snails
3 tbsp parsley, chopped
1/2 C. walnuts, toasted in a pan, chopped
4 tbsp Parmigiano-Reggiano cheese
1 tbsp black pepper,
1/2 tsp salt

Directions

1. Prepare the spaghetti by following the instructions on the package. Drain it. Place a pan over medium heat. Heat in it the oil. Cook in it the onion with mushroom for 5 to 6 min.

2. Stir in the anchovies with garlic. Cook them for 1 min.

3. Get a mixing bowl: Whisk in it the corn flour with lime juice. Stir it into the pan with the crème fraiche.

4. Cook them for 1 to 2 min over low heat. Stir in the snails. Let the sauce cook until it becomes slightly thick.

5. Turn off the heat. Stir in the parsley, walnuts, Parmesan and pepper. Season it with some salt and pepper to make the snail sauce. Stir the spaghetti into the snail sauce and coat it with it.

6. Serve it hot with some extra cheese and chopped herbs.

7. Enjoy.

SEATTLE
Fruit Spaghetti with Pears

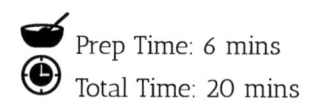

Prep Time: 6 mins

Total Time: 20 mins

Servings per Recipe: 2

Calories	751.7
Fat	28.4g
Cholesterol	18.7mg
Sodium	434.6mg
Carbohydrates	100.3g
Protein	27.7g

Ingredients

7 oz. spaghetti
7 oz. baby spinach leaves, washed and chopped
1.5 oz. gorgonzola cheese
1/2 ripe pears, peeled, cored and sliced
1/2 tsp dried thyme

1/2 tsp dried sage
1/2 C. walnuts, shelled, chopped
1 tsp lemon juice
fresh ground black pepper,

Directions

1. Prepare the spaghetti by following the instructions on the package. Drain it.
2. Place a large pot over medium heat. Stir in it the spaghetti with gorgonzola cheese, spinach, a splash of water or milk, a pinch of salt and pepper.
3. Heat it for few minutes. Add more water if the spaghetti is getting dry.
4. Stir in the pear with walnuts, thyme and sage. Heat them for few minutes.
5. Spoon the spaghetti into a serving bowl. Drizzle over it some lemon juice and a pinch of black pepper.
6. Serve it warm with some chopped nuts.
7. Enjoy.

Chili
Tuna and Pasta Casserole

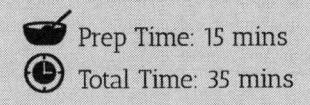 Prep Time: 15 mins

Total Time: 35 mins

Servings per Recipe: 4
Calories	920.9
Fat	38.3g
Cholesterol	76.6mg
Sodium	402.8mg
Carbohydrates	108.6g
Protein	34.0g

Ingredients

500 g spaghetti
2 tbsp olive oil
2 garlic cloves, peeled and chopped
4 tbsp parsley, chopped
1 anchovy packed in oil, drained and chopped
1/2 red chile, chopped
200 g tuna in vegetable oil

1 lemon, juice
125 g butter
fresh parmesan cheese
salt
fresh black pepper

Directions

1. Prepare the spaghetti by following the instructions on the package. Drain it.
2. Place a pan over medium heat. Heat in it the oil. Cook in it the parsley with garlic for 1 min.
3. Stir in the anchovies, chili and tuna. Cook them for 2 min.
4. Stir in the lemon juice and turn off the heat.
5. Stir in the spaghetti with butter, a pinch of salt and pepper.
6. Transfer the spaghetti to a serving bowl. Top it with some grated parmesan then serve it warm.
7. Enjoy.

SATURDAY NIGHT
Veggie Spaghetti with Mushrooms

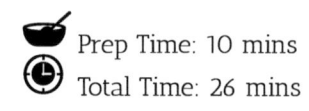 Prep Time: 10 mins

Total Time: 26 mins

Servings per Recipe: 6
Calories	163.0
Fat	4.3g
Cholesterol	0.0mg
Sodium	436.8mg
Carbohydrates	31.9g
Protein	4.2g

Ingredients

4 lbs. spaghetti squash
2 C. fresh tomatoes, chopped
1 C. fresh mushrooms, sliced
1 C. green pepper, diced
1/2 C. carrot, shredded
1/4 C. red onion, diced
2 garlic cloves, minced
2 tsp Italian seasoning

1/8 tsp pepper
1 tbsp olive oil
1 (15 oz.) cans tomato sauce
parmesan cheese, grated

Directions

1. Slice the squash in half and discard the seeds. Place it with the cut up side facing down in the microwave.
2. Cook it for 15 to 17 min on high. Allow it to cool for few minutes then shred it.
3. Place a pan over medium heat. Heat in it the oil.
4. Cook in it the tomatoes, mushrooms, green pepper, carrot, onion, garlic, Italian seasoning and pepper for 7 min.
5. Stir in the tomato sauce and cook them for 2 to 3 min. Add the spaghetti squash and toss it to coat.
6. Serve your spaghetti hot with some grated parmesan cheese.
7. Enjoy

Spaghetti and Meatballs

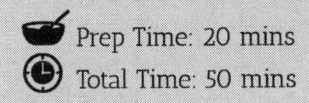

Prep Time: 20 mins
Total Time: 50 mins

Servings per Recipe: 6

Calories	491.3
Fat	11.5g
Cholesterol	86.8mg
Sodium	604.0mg
Carbohydrates	71.6g
Protein	31.4g

Ingredients

Sauce
1 tbsp olive oil
1 medium onion, chopped
4 garlic cloves, minced
3 tbsp tomato paste
1 (28 oz.) cans crushed fire-roasted tomatoes
1 tsp minced adobo seasoning
2 tsp chopped oregano leaves
1 sprig fresh rosemary
salt
1/4 C. torn fresh basil leaf
Meat
cooking spray
1 lb. ground turkey

1 slice whole wheat bread, crusts removed, crumbed
1/4 C. grated parmesan cheese
1/2 C. grated carrot
1/2 C. chopped onion
2 large garlic cloves, minced
2 tbsp minced fresh parsley leaves
2 tsp minced fresh thyme leaves
1 egg, lightly beaten
1/2 tsp salt
fresh ground black pepper
1 (16 oz.) boxes whole wheat spaghetti

Directions

1. Prepare the spaghetti by following the instructions on the package. Drain it.
2. To make the sauce:
3. Place a large saucepan over medium heat. Heat in it the oil. Cook in it the onion for 4 min.
4. Stir in the garlic and cook them for 2 min. Stir in the tomato paste, tomatoes, chipotles, oregano, rosemary, and salt.
5. Cook them until they start boiling. Lower the heat and let them cook for an extra 16 min.
6. To make the meatballs:
7. Before you do anything, preheat the oven broiler. Grease a baking sheet and place it aside.

8. Get a mixing bowl: Mix in it all the meatballs ingredients. Shape it into 2 inches meatballs.
9. Place the meatballs on the greased baking sheet. Cook them in the oven for 11 min.
10. Drain the rosemary sprig from the sauce. Stir into it the basil with meatballs.
11. Put on the lid and let them cook for 12 min over low medium heat.
12. Place the spaghetti in serving bowls. Spoon over it the meatballs sauce then serve them hot.
13. Enjoy.

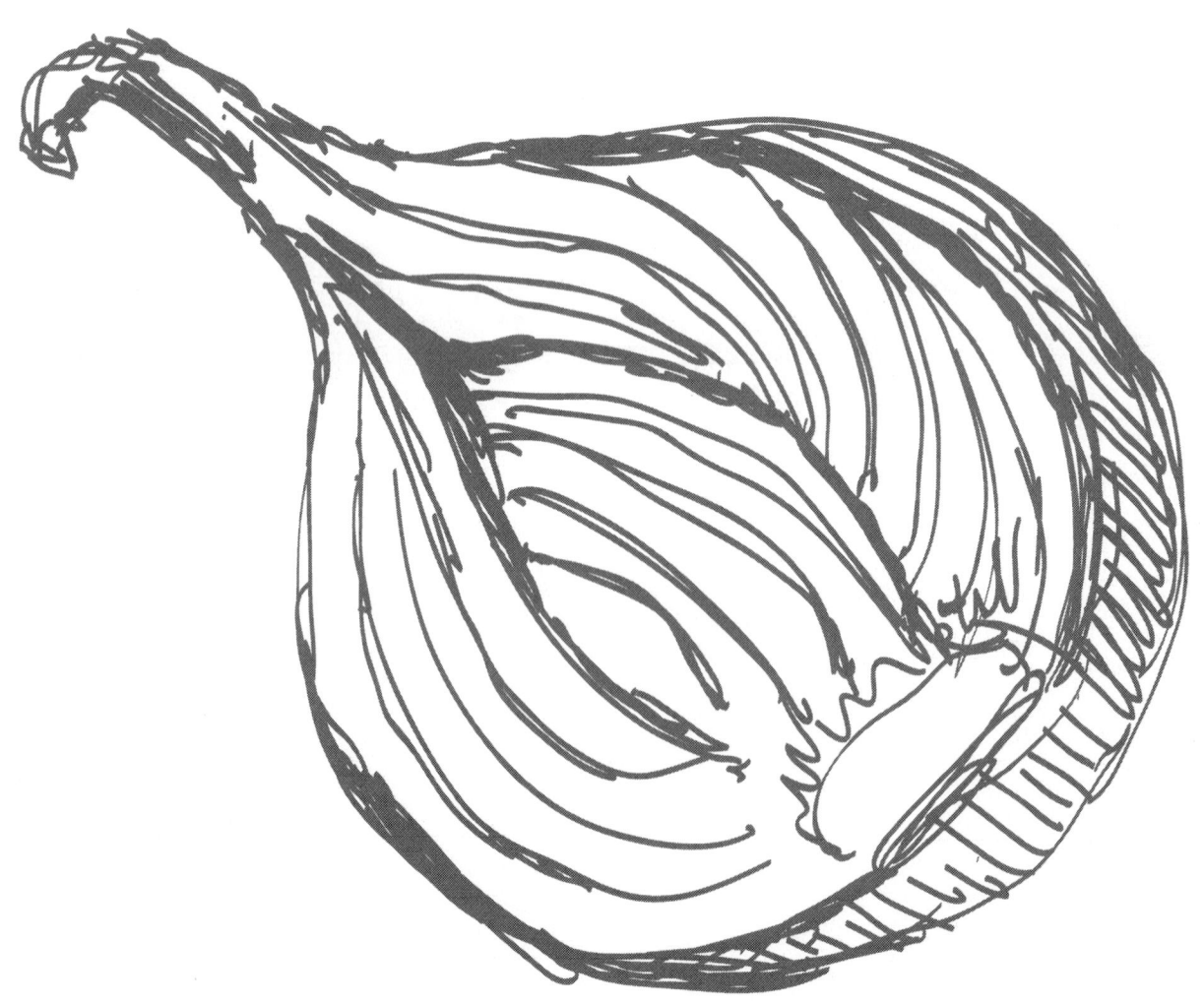

Tropical
Shrimp and Pasta Pockets

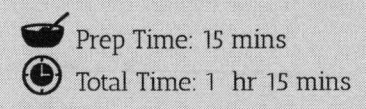 Prep Time: 15 mins

Total Time: 1 hr 15 mins

Servings per Recipe: 6

Calories	204.7
Fat	5.8g
Cholesterol	5.4mg
Sodium	1309.8mg
Carbohydrates	32.8g
Protein	5.5g

Ingredients

1 medium spaghetti squash
2 tsp olive oil
2 tsp sea salt
2 C. pasta sauce
1/2 C. chopped fresh pineapple, chopped
1/2 C. chopped cocktail shrimp, chopped

6 mini pita pockets
1/4 C. arugula
1 oz. goat cheese

Directions

1. Before you do anything, preheat the oven to 350 F.
2. Get a small mixing bowl: Toss in it the shrimp with pineapple.
3. Slice the squash in half and discard the seeds. Drizzle over them 1 tsp of olive oil and a pinch salt.
4. Lay the squash halves on a lined up baking tray. Lay a loose piece of foil over them to cover them.
5. Cook them in the oven for 60 min. Allow them to cool down for few minutes then shred them.
6. Get a mixing bowl: Toss the squash with 1 3/4 up of pasta sauce in a microwave safe bowl.
7. Heat them in the microwave for few minutes.
8. Spoon the mixture into the pita pockets.
9. Top them with the shrimp and pineapple mix, followed by the arugula, pasta sauce, and goat cheese.
10. Serve your spaghetti pockets right away.
11. Enjoy.

CHICKEN
Spaghetti with Southern Barbecued Sauce

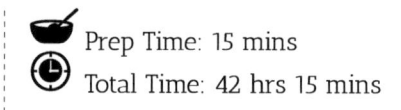

Prep Time: 15 mins
Total Time: 42 hrs 15 mins

Servings per Recipe: 6
Calories	640.1
Fat	10.8g
Cholesterol	63.4mg
Sodium	972.9mg
Carbohydrates	103.1g
Protein	32.8g

Ingredients

1 tbsp olive oil
1 small green bell pepper, chopped
1/2 yellow onion
1 tbsp garlic salt
1 lb. beef cooked and chopped
1 lb. spaghetti
Sauce
2 C. ketchup
1 C. water
1/2 C. apple cider vinegar

5 tbsp light brown sugar
5 tbsp sugar
1/2 tbsp fresh ground black pepper
1/2 tbsp onion powder
1/2 tbsp ground mustard
1 tbsp lemon juice
1 tbsp Worcestershire sauce

Directions

1. To make the barbecue sauce: Place a heavy saucepan over medium heat. Stir in it all the barbecue sauce ingredients. Cook them until they start boiling. Lower the heat and let them cook for 120 min over low heat until it thickens.
2. To make the spaghetti: Place a pan over medium heat. Heat in it the oil. Cook in it the onion with pepper for 3 min.
3. Add the garlic with a pinch of salt. Stir in the 2 1/2 C. of the barbecue sauce.
4. Cook them until they start boiling. Lower the heat and stir in it the chopped chicken.
5. Let it cook for few more minutes. Stir in the spaghetti and toss them to coat. Serve it hot. Enjoy.

 *Ice Cream*
"Pasta"

🥣 Prep Time: 10 mins
🕐 Total Time: 10 mins

Servings per Recipe: 1	
Calories	819.0
Fat	35.9g
Cholesterol	106.2mg
Sodium	325.7mg
Carbohydrates	120.8g
Protein	11.8g

Ingredients

1 1/2 C. vanilla ice cream
1/4-1/2 C. strawberry ice cream topping
1/4-1/2 C. chocolate ice cream,
2 tbsp   chopped nuts

2 - 3 fresh mint leaves

Directions

1. Place the 3 ice creams aside to sit for few minutes until they become soft.
2. Place the vanilla ice cream in a potato rice and press it into a serving bowl in a swirly motion like spaghetti.
3. Use an ice cream spoon to scoop balls of the chocolate ice cream. Lay them over the vanilla ice cream like spaghetti.
4. Drizzle the strawberry ice cream topping over them to make the sauce.
5. Garnish them with the chopped nuts and mint leaves.
6. Serve your spaghetti ice cream right away.
7. Enjoy.

BLACK BEAN
and Mushroom Pasta with Pepper and Basil

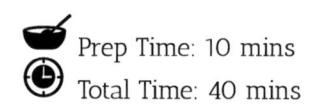 Prep Time: 10 mins

Total Time: 40 mins

Servings per Recipe: 6

Calories	524.0
Fat	12.3g
Cholesterol	14.6mg
Sodium	457.9mg
Carbohydrates	79.6g
Protein	26.0g

Ingredients

1 large onion, chopped
1 (8 oz.) packages sliced fresh mushrooms
4 cloves garlic, crushed
1 sweet red pepper, strips
2 tbsp olive oil
2 (15 oz.) cans black beans, rinsed and drained
1 (28 oz.) cans whole tomatoes, undrained and chopped

1 (2 1/4 oz.) cans sliced ripe olives, drained
1/2 tsp dried basil
1/4 tsp salt
1/2 tsp pepper
1 (12 oz.) packages dried spaghetti
1 C. grated parmesan cheese

Directions

1. Prepare the spaghetti by following the instructions on the package. Drain it.
2. Place a large saucepan over medium heat. Heat in it the oil.
3. Cook in it the onion with mushroom, garlic and pepper for 6 min.
4. Stir in the black beans with olives, tomato, basil, salt and pepper.
5. Cook them until they start boiling. Lower the heat and let them cook for 22 min.
6. Spoon the sauce over the spaghetti. Serve it hot with grated parmesan.
7. Enjoy.

Spaghetti
Squash Grillers

🍳 Prep Time: 20 mins
🕐 Total Time: 1 hr 20 mins

Servings per Recipe: 6
Calories	267.8
Fat	18.2g
Cholesterol	59.7mg
Sodium	1239.2mg
Carbohydrates	11.9g
Protein	16.0g

Ingredients

1 medium spaghetti squash
3 tsp olive oil
2 tsp sea salt
1 lb. Italian link sausage, chunks
12 medium size shrimp
12 baby bella mushrooms

12 inches fresh pineapple chunks
1 C. Ragú® Pasta Sauce
1 medium sweet onion
6 stalks celery, bokchoy
1 oz. feta cheese, crumbled

Directions

1. Before you do anything, preheat the oven to 350 F.
2. Slice the squash in half. Drizzle over it 1 tsp of olive oil. Season it with some salt and pepper.
3. Place the squash halves on a baking tray. Lay a piece of foil over the squash halves to cover them.
4. Cook them in the oven for 60 min. Allow them to cool down for few minutes. Shred them.
5. Before you do anything, preheat grill and grease it.
6. Thread the sausage chunks with onion, pineapple, mushroom, and shrimp into skewers while alternating between them.
7. Coat them with the rest of the olive oil. Grill the kabobs for 3 to 5 min.
8. Place a pan over medium heat. Toss in it the spaghetti squash with 3/4 C. of ragu sauce. Heat them for 5 min.
9. Lay the bokchoy stalks on a serving plate. Pour over the spaghetti.
10. Lay the sausage kabobs on top followed by the remaining ragu sauce and feta cheese.
11. Serve it right away.
12. Enjoy.

TEX-MEX
Spaghetti

🥣 Prep Time: 30 mins
🕐 Total Time: 45 mins

Servings per Recipe: 4
Calories   580.5
Fat   7.0g
Cholesterol   204.7mg
Sodium   939.8mg
Carbohydrates   89.6g
Protein   37.9g

Ingredients

375 g spaghetti
1 tbsp extra virgin olive oil
4 garlic cloves, sliced
1/4 tsp chili flakes
650 g prawns

6 tomatoes, chopped
2 tbsp parsley, chopped

Directions

1. Prepare the spaghetti by following the instructions on the package. Drain it. Reserve 1/2 C. of the cooking liquid.

2. Place a pan over medium heat. Heat in it the oil. Cook in it the garlic with chili for 2 min.

3. Stir in the prawns then cook for 3 to 4 min. Stir in the tomato with the reserved liquid. Let them cook for 2 to 3 min.

4. Add the spaghetti with parsley, a pinch of salt and pepper. Toss them to coat.

5. Serve your spaghetti hot right away.

6. Enjoy.

Spaghetti Marrakesh

🍳 Prep Time: 10 mins
🕐 Total Time: 30 mins

Servings per Recipe: 4
Calories   247.7
Fat   14.2g
Cholesterol   30.5mg
Sodium   516.2mg
Carbohydrates   32.2g
Protein   3.2g

Ingredients

4 lbs. spaghetti squash
4 tbsp unsalted butter, cut into pieces
2 garlic cloves, minced
1 tsp ground cumin
1/2 tsp ground coriander
1/8 tsp cayenne

3/4 tsp salt
2 tbsp fresh cilantro, chopped

Directions

1. Use a knife or a fork to pierce the squash several times. Place it in the microwave and let it cook for 8 min on high.
2. Flip the squash and cook it for an extra 9 min on high. Let it cool down for few minutes then shred it.
3. Place a saucepan over medium heat. Heat in it the butter until it melt. Sauté in it the garlic for 45 sec.
4. Add the spices and mix them well. Turn off the heat. Stir the spaghetti into the spicy butter mixture.
5. Serve it hot with some grated cheese.
6. Enjoy.

CAST IRON
Spaghetti

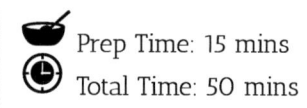
Prep Time: 15 mins
Total Time: 50 mins

Servings per Recipe: 6
Calories	278.8
Fat	7.5g
Cholesterol	65.0mg
Sodium	428.3mg
Carbohydrates	31.3g
Protein	21.9g

Ingredients

1/2 tsp olive oil
1 lb. ground chicken, skinless
1/2 C. onion, chopped
1/2 C. bell pepper, chopped
15 oz. tomato sauce

4 C. water
1 envelope taco seasoning mix
8 oz. thin spaghetti, uncooked
1/2 C. fat-free cheddar cheese, shredded

Directions

1. Place a pan over medium heat. Heat in it the oil. Cook in it the chicken, onion, and bell pepper for 8 min.
2. Add the water, tomato sauce and taco seasoning mix. Cook them until they start boiling.
3. Lower the heat and stir in the pasta. Put on the lid and let them cook for 26 min.
4. Serve your taco spaghetti hot with grated cheddar cheese.
5. Enjoy.

Mirepoix
Soup

🥣 Prep Time: 20 mins
🕐 Total Time: 1 hr 40 mins

Servings per Recipe: 15	
Calories	34.6
Fat	1.3g
Cholesterol	0.0mg
Sodium	21.0mg
Carbohydrates	5.5g
Protein	1.1g

Ingredients

2 lbs. spaghetti squash
1 tbsp vegetable oil
2 C. mirepoix
3 garlic cloves, minced
10 oz. portabella mushrooms, sliced
1 (28 oz.) cans tomatoes with basil

8 C. vegetable broth
1 1/2 tbsp fresh thyme, minced
6 oz. Baby Spinach
salt and pepper

Directions

1. Use a knife or a fork to pierce the squash several times. Place it in the microwave and let it cook for 6 min on high.
2. Flip the squash and cook it for an extra 7 min on high. Let it cool down for few minutes then shred it.
3. Place a large pot over medium heat. Heat in it the oil. Cook in it the mirepoix for 4 min.
4. Stir in the mushroom with garlic. Cook them for 3 min. Add the tomato and cook them for 9 min.
5. Stir in the stock. Lower the heat then let them cook for 22 min.
6. Add the thyme with spaghetti squash, a pinch of salt and pepper. Let them cook for 6 min.
7. Stir in the spinach and cook them for an extra 3 min.
8. Serve your spaghetti soup hot.
9. Enjoy.

ALTERNATIVE
Fruit Salad

Prep Time: 25 mins
Total Time: 34 mins

Servings per Recipe: 12
Calories	241.4
Fat	7.6g
Cholesterol	35.2mg
Sodium	115.3mg
Carbohydrates	40.5g
Protein	4.5g

Ingredients

1 C. confectioners' sugar
2 eggs
1/2 C. lemon juice
1/2 tsp salt
1/2 lb. spaghetti, broken into pieces
1 (20 oz.) cans pineapple
3 medium tart apples, diced

1 (8 oz.) cartons frozen whipped topping, thawed
1/4 C. walnuts, chopped
maraschino cherry, halved

Directions

1. Prepare the spaghetti by following the instructions on the package. Drain it.
2. Before you do anything, preheat the oven to 450 F. Grease a baking sheet and place it aside.
3. Place a large saucepan over medium heat. Stir in it the sugar, eggs, lemon juice and salt. Let them cook for 4 to 5 min.
4. Turn off the heat and let the sauce cool down completely.
5. Get a serving bowl: Toss in it the spaghetti with pineapple juice and apples. Drain them.
6. Add the lemon sauce with pineapple. Put on the lid and place the salad in the fridge for an overnight.
7. Stir in the whipped topping. Top the salad with cherries and walnuts then serve it right away.
8. Enjoy.

Pasta Torte

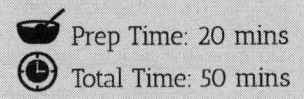 Prep Time: 20 mins
Total Time: 50 mins

Servings per Recipe: 6

Calories	438.3
Fat	11.2g
Cholesterol	30.6mg
Sodium	350.6mg
Carbohydrates	59.9g
Protein	23.0g

Ingredients

1 lb. uncooked spaghetti
1/2 C. grated parmesan cheese
1/2 C. ricotta cheese
1 tbsp Italian seasoning
4 egg whites
1/4 C. chopped fresh basil

2 tomatoes, chopped
4 slices provolone cheese, cut into fourths

Directions

1. Before you do anything, preheat the oven to 350 F.
2. Prepare the spaghetti by following the instructions on the package. Drain it.
3. Get a mixing bowl: Toss in it the spaghettis with parmesan, ricotta cheese, Italian seasoning and egg whites.
4. Pour half of the mixture into the greased pan. Top it with half of the basil followed by the tomato slices and provolone cheese.
5. Repeat the process to make another layer. Place the pan in the oven and cook them for 16 min.
6. Serve your tart hot.
7. Enjoy.

SPAGHETTI
Rustica

Prep Time: 15 mins
Total Time: 1 hr 15 mins

Servings per Recipe: 2
Calories	1081.3
Fat	39.4g
Cholesterol	153.8mg
Sodium	2698.6mg
Carbohydrates	130.8g
Protein	52.9g

Ingredients

2 boneless chicken breasts, diced
1/4 C. plain flour
1 tsp salt
1/4 C. butter, melted
1 celery, chopped
1 onion, chopped
1 garlic clove, pressed
2 carrots, strips
2 small yellow squash, sliced

1 (8 oz.) tomato sauce
1 (14 oz.) tomatoes, diced
1/2 tsp sugar
1 1/2 C. water
8 oz. spaghetti noodles
4 C. water
1/2 tsp salt

Directions

1. Season the chicken pieces with a pinch of salt then toss them in flour.
2. Place a pot over medium heat. Heat in it the butter. Cook in it the chicken pieces for 4 min.
3. Drain them and place them aside. Stir in the onion with garlic and celery. Cook them for 4 min.
4. Add the chicken back with carrots, squash, tomato sauce, sugar, diced tomato and 1 1/2 C. of water.
5. Put on the lid and let them cook for 35 to 42 min. Adjust the seasoning of the sauce.
6. Serve it hot over the spaghetti with some grated cheese.
7. Enjoy.

Pesto Spaghetti

Prep Time: 15 mins
Total Time: 25 mins

Servings per Recipe: 4
Calories	1673.4
Fat	93.8g
Cholesterol	51.8mg
Sodium	453.8mg
Carbohydrates	167.3g
Protein	42.9g

Ingredients

1 1/2 C. chopped parsley
4 tbsp chopped basil
salt
pepper
1 garlic clove
2 oz. ground almonds
2 oz. walnuts

1 C. oil
3 oz. grated parmesan cheese
26.5 oz. spaghetti
2 oz. butter
parmesan cheese

Directions

1. Prepare the spaghetti by following the instructions on the package. Drain it.
2. Get a food processor: Place in it the parsley, basil, salt, pepper, crushed garlic, almonds, walnuts and oil. Blend them smooth.
3. Get a mixing bowl: Stir in it the butter with the hot pasta.
4. Stir in the pesto sauce with a pinch of salt and pepper.
5. Sprinkle some parmesan cheese on top. Serve it right away.
6. Enjoy.

MEDITERRANEAN
Spaghetti

Prep Time: 15 mins
Total Time: 1 hr 15 mins

Servings per Recipe: 6

Calories	633.9
Fat	27.7g
Cholesterol	82.3mg
Sodium	914.1mg
Carbohydrates	65.9g
Protein	30.8g

Ingredients

8 small roma tomatoes
2 tbsp olive oil
1 tbsp balsamic vinegar
2 garlic cloves, halved
1 lb. lamb tenderloin
2 tbsp butter
2 C. breadcrumbs

2 garlic cloves
8 oz. spaghetti
1/2 C. black olives
1 C. feta cheese
12 oz. artichoke hearts

Directions

1. Before you do anything, preheat the oven to 450 F.
2. Slice the squash in half. Place them on a lined up baking sheet.
3. Season them with some salt then pour over them 1 tbsp of oil. Place the pan in the oven then cook them for 22 min
4. Get a blender: Combine in it the 1 tbsp of olive oil with tomato, vinegar, and garlic. Blend them smooth.
5. Get a mixing bowl: Heat in it a splash of oil. Cook in it the lamb tenderloin for 3 to 5 min on each side.
6. Turn off the heat and put on the lid. Let it sit for 6 min. Cut it into thin slices.
7. Prepare the spaghetti by following the instructions on the package.
8. Get a large serving bowl: Combine in it the sliced lamb with spaghetti, olives, feta cheese and artichoke hearts.
9. Drizzle the tomato sauce on top. Sprinkle the breadcrumbs on top.
10. Serve your salad right away.
11. Enjoy.

Pricilla's Primavera

🍳 Prep Time: 50 mins
🕐 Total Time: 50 mins

Servings per Recipe: 4
Calories	1083.7
Fat	60.5g
Cholesterol	80.8mg
Sodium	307.4mg
Carbohydrates	110.7g
Protein	30.8g

Ingredients

1 lb. broccoli, cut into florets
2 small zucchini, diced
4 asparagus spears, trimmed, chopped
1 1/2 C. green beans, trimmed and cut into lengths
1/2 C. green peas
3/4 C. pea pods
1 tbsp canola oil
2 C. mushrooms, sliced
salt & ground black pepper
1 tsp red chilies
1/4 C. parsley, chopped
6 tbsp olive oil
1 tsp garlic, chopped
1/4 C. fresh basil, chopped
3 C. tomatoes, ripe, peeled, seeded, cut into chunks
1 lb. spaghetti
4 tbsp unsalted butter
2 tbsp unsalted chicken stock
1/2 C. heavy cream
2/3 C. Parmigiano-Reggiano cheese, grated
1/3 C. pine nuts

Directions

1. Prepare the spaghetti by following the instructions on the package.
2. Bring a large pot of water to a boil. Cook in it the broccoli, zucchini, asparagus and green beans for 5 min separately.
3. Drain them and place them aside.
4. Place a large pan over medium heat. Heat in it the canola oil. Cook in it the mushroom with a pinch of salt and pepper for 3 min.
5. Get a large mixing bowl: Toss in it the cooked green veggies with mushrooms, chili and parsley. Place it aside.
6. Place a large saucepan over medium heat. Heat in it 3 tbsp of olive oil. Cook in it the garlic with tomato for 5 min.
7. Stir in the basil with a pinch of salt and pepper to make the sauce. Turn off the heat and

put on the lid.

8. Place a large skillet over medium heat. Heat in it the butter. Stir in the broth with cream and parmesan cheese.

9. Let them cook for few minutes until they become smooth. Stir in the spaghetti with half of the veggies.

10. Add the remaining veggies mix with pinenuts. Toss them to coat.

11. Divide the spaghetti veggies between serving bowls. Drizzle the tomato sauce on top with some cheese.

12. Serve it hot.

13. Enjoy.

Alaskan Forest
Creamy Spaghetti

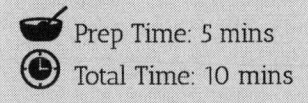 Prep Time: 5 mins

Total Time: 10 mins

Servings per Recipe: 2

Calories	532.7
Fat	26.3g
Cholesterol	143.1mg
Sodium	130.6mg
Carbohydrates	61.7g
Protein	12.8g

Ingredients

2 fish roe, tarako, or pollock
6 oz. spaghetti noodles
2 tbsp butter

1/4 C. heavy cream
1/4 sheet nori, strips

Directions

1. Discard the fish roe casing.
2. Prepare the spaghetti by following the instructions on the package.
3. Place a pan over medium heat. Heat in it the butter. Cook in it the fish roe for 3 to 5 min.
4. Add half of the heavy cream and mix them well. Stir in the remaining cream with pinch of salt and pepper.
5. Add the pasta to the creamy roe sauce and stir it well.
6. Spoon it into serving bowl. Garnish it with nori strips. Serve it hot.
7. Enjoy.

PASTA
Toasters

Prep Time: 5 mins
Total Time: 5 mins

Servings per Recipe: 1
Calories   133.0
Fat   1.6g
Cholesterol   0.0mg
Sodium   340.5mg
Carbohydrates   25.3g
Protein   3.8g

Ingredients

2 slices bread, toasted
7 oz. canned spaghetti and sauce

Directions

1. Toast the bread.
2. Place a small pan over medium heat. Heat in it the spaghetti for few minutes.
3. Slice the toast into 3 triangles. Spoon the spaghetti over them.
4. Garnish them with some grated cheese and chopped parsley. Serve them right away.
5. Enjoy.

Spaghetti Levantine

Prep Time: 10 mins
Total Time: 20 mins

Servings per Recipe: 6
Calories   217.4
Fat   5.6g
Cholesterol   0.0mg
Sodium   787.7mg
Carbohydrates   36.9g
Protein   6.4g

Ingredients

2 tbsp olive oil
2 green bell peppers, cleaned, halved and sliced
2 red bell peppers, cleaned, halved and sliced
2 yellow onions, halved and sliced

16 oz. canned tomato sauce
1 tsp salt
1/4 tsp pepper
1 lb. cooked spaghetti

Directions

1. Prepare the spaghetti by following the instructions on the package.
2. Place a pan over medium heat. Heat in it the oil. Cook in it the onion for 4 min.
3. Stir in the peppers and cook them for 3 min. Add the tomato sauce with a pinch of salt and pepper.
4. Cook them until they start boiling. Lower the heat and let the sauce cook for 11 min.
5. Stir the spaghetti into the sauce and toss them to coat. Serve it hot.
6. Enjoy.

ENJOY THE RECIPES?

KEEP ON COOKING
WITH 6 MORE FREE COOKBOOKS!

Visit our website and simply enter your email address to join the club and receive your 6 cookbooks.

http://booksumo.com/magnet

https://www.instagram.com/booksumopress/

https://www.facebook.com/booksumo/

Printed in Great Britain
by Amazon

13858755R00066